GOOD FOR YOU

GOOD FOR YOU

Bold Flavors with Benefits

100 recipes for gluten-free, dairy-free, vegetarian, and vegan diets

AKHTAR NAWAB
with Andrea Strong

Photographs by
Antonis Achilleos

CHRONICLE BOOKS
SAN FRANCISCO

Library of Congress Cataloging-in-Publication Data

Names: Nawab, Akhtar, author. | Strong, Andrea, author. |
    Achilleos, Antonis, photographer.
Title: Good for you : bold flavors with benefits : 100 recipes for gluten-
    free, dairy-free, vegetarian, and vegan diets / Akhtar Nawab with
    Andrea Strong ; photographs by Antonis Achilleos.
Description: San Francisco, CA : Chronicle Books, 2020. | Includes index.
Identifiers: LCCN 2019051407 | ISBN 9781452181776 (hardcover) |
    ISBN 9781452182179 (ebook)
Subjects: LCSH: International cooking. | Cooking, Indic. | Low-fat diet—
    Recipes. | Vegetarian cooking.
Classification: LCC TX725.A1 N39 2020 | DDC 641.5/63—dc23
    LC record available at https://lccn.loc.gov/2019051407

Manufactured in China.

MIX
Paper from
responsible sources
FSC™ C104723

Prop styling by Mindi Shapiro.
Food styling by Chelsea Zimmer.
Design by Vanessa Dina.
Typesetting by Frank Brayton. Typeset in Intervogue.

10 9 8 7 6 5 4 3 2 1

Chronicle books and gifts are available at special quantity discounts
to corporations, professional associations, literacy programs, and other
organizations. For details and discount information, please contact our
premiums department at corporatesales@chroniclebooks.com or at
1-800-759-0190.

Chronicle Books LLC
680 Second Street
San Francisco, California 94107
www.chroniclebooks.com

GF = GLUTEN FREE
DF = DAIRY FREE
VG = VEGETARIAN
V = VEGAN

FOREWORD

I've always been interested in health and wellness. It took me a while to really understand the impact that healthy eating has on overall well-being. In the 1980s and 1990s, I collected fad diet books and was convinced I would find the key to good health (and a perfect body) in them. A lot of those diets were about loading up on a certain type of food rather than eating a balanced diet.

While working as a makeup artist, I've been responsible for making women (and men) look and feel their best. And while I know the power of a good concealer or red lipstick, what goes into your body has an even bigger impact on how we look on the outside.

I started to pay more attention to what I was eating—both when I was working on the set of a photo shoot and when I was at home taking care of my growing family—and made the connection between the foods I was consuming and how they made me feel.

When I was drinking a lot of water, eating fresh produce, and adding lean proteins, I had more energy and better focus, and I just felt better. When I ditched the processed foods and sugary snacks, I immediately noticed my skin was clearer, my eyes were brighter, and my hair was shinier. I tossed those diet books and started to seek out the advice of nutritionists, functional medicine doctors, and personal trainers who helped me shift my lifestyle.

For many people, a healthy diet isn't associated with good flavor. It's associated with steamed broccoli and poached chicken with no salt. Bland and boring. Often, the focus is on what you can't have, making it feel like punishment instead of nourishment. Sometimes healthy eating just gets a bad rap.

I first met Akhtar Nawab when he was developing recipes for the restaurant Indie Fresh. He proved to me that healthy food doesn't have to be bland and flavorless. It doesn't have to be boring. He's infused his recipes with a rich combination of spices and flavors that reflect his Indian heritage and diverse culinary background. I immediately fell in love with his vision of food that is good for you while also tasting delicious.

Akhtar's approach also had an impact on how I cook at home. I can whip up a fast meal with good-for-you ingredients that's robust enough to feed a family of hungry boys, and I can invite my team over for lunch and know they're going to feel energized—not sluggish—after we eat together.

The skills, tips, and recipes packed into this book are essential for any home chef. Akhtar's simple and healthy recipes—like Cauliflower Pizza Crust and Pumpkin Protein Pancakes—are the kind you'll keep coming back to. His approach is modern, thoughtful, and diverse without leaving you with cabinets full of ingredients you'll never use again. And if you're a visual person like me, you won't be able to get enough of the beautiful, mouthwatering imagery.

Everyone has a different journey when it comes to health and wellness. It takes time and a lot of trial and error to find what is going to work for you, your body, and your lifestyle. If you're just getting started, I can't think of a better place to begin than with these recipes and techniques from Akhtar.

—**Bobbi Brown**

INTRODUCTION

Most stories have a clear beginning, a place where everything starts. But my story—the one about an Indian kid from Kentucky who ends up becoming a classically trained chef known for American, Mexican, Italian, and, of all things, healthy cooking—is kind of complicated.

I could start in the 1970s in Louisville, where I grew up, a first-generation son of Indian parents in a town marked by white bread and *The Brady Bunch*, who spent weekends in the kitchen cooking saag paneer and keema with my mom, my clothes saturated with the aroma of cumin, cardamom, and ginger.

Or I could begin when I dropped out of college and took a job at Domino's Pizza because I had no idea what I wanted to do—other than I was fairly certain I didn't want to follow in the footsteps of every one of my immediate and distant relatives and become a doctor.

Then again, I often think my story really started when I landed in New York City and began cooking for Tom Colicchio at Gramercy Tavern, the ground floor of the American food revolution. Under Tom, I learned so much about food and cooking—about seasonality, local farmers, and how to coax the most flavor from the simplest of ingredients.

Over the dozen or so years since my beginning at Gramercy Tavern, I have cooked nearly every kind of food at every kind of restaurant: inspired Italian at Craft and Craftbar; modern Indian at my first solo project, Elettaria; nutrition-forward fast casual at Indie Fresh; my own offbeat brand of Mexican at Alta Calidad and Otra Vez; and more refined seasonal American fare at Prather's on the Alley in Washington, DC.

While my journey has been anything but linear, what it has lacked in predictability it has well made up for with passion and learning and lots of cooking. I feel more at peace and more content both in the kitchen and at home than I've ever felt in my life. It's been a journey—a strange, awesome, twisted, and incredibly hard one.

Which brings us here, to this book, *Good for You*, and my mission, which is to cook and serve food that's not missing anything and that's also, as the title suggests, good for you. With all my varied experiences, why focus on healthful food?

When I think about it, part of the reason definitely goes back to my childhood, when, I'll be honest with you, I was a chubby kid. Perhaps it's because my mom, who is from Northern India, is such a great cook. I remember her wood-paneled kitchen as my own full-service Indian home-cooking restaurant, where heaping dishes of korma and keema, aromatic pots of jasmine rice, and platters of steamy roti were ferried out to the dining room with wonderful regularity. Which is probably why I was the overweight kid in elementary school. I did slim down playing soccer in middle school and high school, but when I went to college I fell into what most college kids do: I partied and I gained a ton of weight. Forget the freshman 15. I put on the freshman 50! After my freshman year of college, I topped out around 250 pounds [113 kg]. I went home to Louisville, Kentucky, for the summer and I never went back. (It wasn't the weight; that style of learning just wasn't for me.) Instead, I tried to get my act together.

I met with a nutritionist who put me on a joyless (but effective) diet for a year and a half. It was so bad that I can still remember every meal, scenes from some sort of recurring culinary nightmare. I started each day with 1 cup [226 g] of unsweetened shredded wheat, half a banana, and ½ cup [120 ml] of skim milk. A morning snack would be a slice or two of low-fat white cheese and an apple. For lunch, I made a low-fat cheese sandwich on this whole-wheat bread that was so thin and dry it was practically a cracker. I was permitted 1 tsp of mustard; otherwise I think I would have choked. An afternoon snack was ¼ cup [60 g] of unsweetened nonfat yogurt. For dinner, I was permitted 4 oz [115 g] of lean protein cooked without any fat, plus 3 oz [85 g] of carbohydrates—usually steamed brown rice.

Combined with rigorous exercise, the plan worked. Thankfully, the thinking behind healthy eating has evolved, embracing healthy fats like olive oil, salmon, avocado, and nuts—foods that satisfy you for longer periods of time. You can even eat a whole egg, not just the white! In the '80s, it was banishment of all kinds of fat, little regard for whole ingredients (in fact, a lot of reliance on low-calorie processed ingredients that are not at all good for you), and simply an emphasis on shrinking overall caloric intake. It wasn't really healthy—and it definitely wasn't sustainable.

I'm in my forties now, I have a young daughter, and I run several restaurants around the country. Given my age and how busy I am, by most accounts I should have gained weight and slowed down. Yet, over the course of the past twenty years, that hasn't happened. A lot of that is owed to the work I did developing healthful recipes for Indie Fresh, the fast-casual health-conscious restaurant I opened with Shom Chowdhury in 2014. Shom was then the COO of Juice Press and he was looking to open a restaurant focused on fast, fresh, and nutritious food. By that time, I'd already done lots of different kinds of cooking, so I was excited for the opportunity to do something outside of my comfort zone and to develop good-for-you recipes—according to today's updated thinking—that also taste great.

The Indie Fresh concept was challenging because I had to figure out how to cook with gluten- and dairy-free ingredients, something I had never really done. On top of that, the recipes were also tested by an actual nutritionist. So I had to be accountable; there was no fudging of extra olive oil here and a rounded cup of another ingredient there, especially because the recipes had to be simple in order to be scaled up. But I loved the process of puzzling out how to pack flavor and texture into each bite while keeping an eye on the overall nutritional profile of a dish. Gluten-free recipes like the Pumpkin Protein Pancakes (page 66), Morning Glory Muffins (page 62), and bread took dozens of iterations to perfect. At the end of the day, I felt I'd finally figured out a way to make healthy food taste like not-so-healthy food.

I've found that when you take the time to incorporate roasted chiles or toasted spices, you don't miss a lot of the fat that chefs often rely on to make something taste good. You can make lean protein taste amazingly intense and keep it moist with an aromatic brine or a spiced marinade. Fish may need just some olive oil and a smattering of herbs, chiles, and lemon to become an exciting dinner. Mexican food can be super rich and full of queso, but it also leans heavily on healthful nuts, seeds, chiles, and herbs that can impart layers of thrilling flavors that are also gluten free. The same goes for Indian, the cuisine of my childhood. My mom makes a keema muttar, a rich sautéed ground beef dish that's delicious, with a base of buttery ghee. But I change things up, using olive oil instead for a lighter result that's still super flavorful.

Looking into the classic recipes I was trained on at places like Gramercy Tavern, I've also found ways to create creaminess without butter or actual cream. Take the standard French soubise, which is made with julienned onions sweated down in a copious amount of butter and cream. It became an obsession of mine to achieve that rich, smooth texture without butter. What I finally settled on was steaming the julienned onions to remove any bitterness, then simmering them in a pot with almond milk to get that similar texture. I add coriander seeds for brightness before puréeing the whole batch until smooth. This Vegan Soubise (page 26) is the key to the creaminess in all of my soups and sauces. Look at it as a blank yet rich, lushly textured palette for the star flavors of whatever dish it is supporting.

This book is dedicated to cooking (and sharing) clean, healthy food that is simply joyful. I've taken my training from Indie Fresh and applied it to all of the cuisines I cook, which, as I've mentioned, run a rather crazy gamut from Indian and Mexican to Italian and American. As a dad, I also cook for my daughter and her friends, some of whom can be picky, so I have become adept at creating recipes that appeal across the board, for all types of eaters. This book also reflects the way healthful eating has evolved over the years so that it now includes more traditional ethnic cuisines. It's so much easier to source many of these ingredients from places like Whole Foods, Amazon, and even Trader Joe's; that means the dinner table is often a cross-cultural affair.

There are many other secrets tucked inside the pages of this book: what to keep in your pantry, how to achieve flavor without fat, how to make gluten-free bread, why you always (ALWAYS) must toast your spices (even the dry ones!), and many more.

I want to also note here, at the outset, that I'm not a vegan. I'm an omnivore, and I still incorporate meat into my diet, but I tend to make sure it's sustainably produced and on the healthier side, like bison, a protein that's rich in flavor and low in fat. That said, I would say my diet is plant forward and mostly gluten free, because that's what's best for my health and the health of our planet—greenhouse gases emitted from producing livestock and cattle make a significant impact on global warming. So you'll find that many of the recipes here are gluten free, dairy free, vegetarian, or vegan, and will be designated as GF, DF, VG (vegetarian), or V (vegan), as appropriate.

My hope is that once you've had time to cook your way through most of these recipes, you'll be able to easily and joyfully cook food that is intensely delicious and overwhelmingly healthful. You'll hopefully have a lot more energy, and feel better about what you are feeding yourself and your family—food that's good for you!

CHAPTER ONE

FOUND

ATIONS

Cooking is sort of like building a house; you need a strong, solid foundation or everything else will fall apart. That's why this first chapter is so important. These basic recipes—Tomato Paste (page 31), Romesco Sauce (page 33), Cashew Purée (page 37), and more—are the building blocks for so many of the meals you'll find on these pages, from soups to sauces, burgers to meatballs, and more.

My suggestion is to consider these foundation recipes an extension of your pantry. I'd make these staples ahead of time and keep them in the refrigerator or freezer; dividing them into ice cube trays works well for lots of these. This way, you'll have a stockpile on hand, so it's not a chore to make the individual items when you need them for a more complex recipe.

To develop these foundation recipes, many of which are vegan and gluten free, I actually started out with the classic full-fat recipe and then began to strip away what I thought was unnecessary. From there, I replaced whatever I thought was missing with something that would add a nutritional benefit and amplify flavor.

To give you an idea, I went through quite a few unsuccessful variations for the gluten-free recipes in this book; it took a long time to perfect the Gluten-Free Bread (page 46), Gluten-Free Pasta (page 43), and the Gluten-Free Roti (page 45) because those gluten-free flours are tricky and can produce dry, brittle results. In each recipe I found a way to produce a nicer texture by adding yogurt, tapioca, or Cashew Purée (page 37).

I also struggled with my Bison Meatballs with Cremini Mushroom Sauce and Quinoa (page 143). The initial recipes I tested met my nutrition standards, but they tasted like golf balls, and I couldn't serve them with a clear conscience. It wasn't until I created my Cashew Purée (page 37) that I found a way to essentially save my meatballs and turned them from golf balls into something really juicy and delicious.

Aside from the Cashew Purée, this chapter contains many other basics, like my Vegan Soubise (page 26)—essential for soups like the Creamy Broccoli and Coconut Soup (page 97)—and my Tomato Paste (page 31), an important alternative to store-bought tomato paste, which is full of sugar. I also rely on my homemade Tomato Paste for marinades.

Speaking of marinades, I've included a couple of them in this chapter as well: My Mexican Marinade (page 41) that will forever change your weeknight roast chicken and Thanksgiving turkey, and The Best Basic Marinade (page 38) that can be used

on everything from chicken breasts to a delicate piece of fish and even some hearty vegetables, such as butternut squash or Brussels sprouts.

These recipes are wonderful but they do take some time, so feel free to dig into them on a weekend, or use store-bought gluten-free products instead, depending on your mood. In terms of dry goods, you probably have basics like olive oil, kosher salt, pepper, and the like in your pantry, but I've listed anything that these recipes require that's a bit out of the ordinary in the next sections.

OK, that's about all for now. Let's get cooking; your house is waiting.

A to Z Pantry List

Acai juice

Agave

Aji amarillo

Almond flour

Amaranth

Black chickpeas

Black truffle oil

Cacao nibs

Chia seeds

Chickpeas

Cider vinegar

Coconut flour (see Good to Know, facing page)

Coconut milk

Coconut oil

Dates

Dried hijiki

Flaxseed

Gluten-free flour

Hemp hearts (see Good to Know, page 24)

Japanese rice crackers

Koji

Lentils

Maldon sea salt

Maseca

Matcha tea

Persian lime powder

Pumpkin seed oil

Pumpkin seeds

Quinoa

Shredded coconut

Tamari

Tamarind paste

Tapioca starch

Thai red curry paste

Unsalted nuts, such as hazelnuts, almonds, and pistachios

Vegan protein powder, such as hemp or pea (see Good to Know, page 55)

Yuba noodles

Spices

Black cardamom

Black mustard seeds

Cardamom (ground and pods)

Cinnamon sticks

Coriander seeds

Cumin seeds

Curry leaves

Fenugreek leaves

Ground cinnamon

Ground cloves

Ground coriander

Ground cumin

Ground fenugreek

Mexican oregano

Smoked paprika
(also known as pimenton)

Tajin

Turmeric

Chiles

Canned chipotle in adobo

Chile de árbol

Chile piquin

Guajillo

Pasilla

Piquillo peppers

Poblano

Refrigerator Staples

Almond milk

Coconut milk

Kefir

Grass-fed butter

Vegan butter

Bison (see Good to Know, page 87)

GOOD TO KNOW:
Coconut Flour

Coconut flour is a soft, naturally grain- and gluten-free flour made from dried coconut meat. It's a good alternative to almond flour for those who have nut aller-gies, and it adds a nice toasted coconut flavor to anything you're baking. I use it for gluten-free recipes because it helps absorb moisture and adds a little bit of structure. Coconut flour is fairly high in protein, and relatively low in carbohydrates by comparison to other flours. It's rich in manga-nese (which supports bone health and acts as an antioxidant and anti-inflammatory). In addition to manganese, coconut flour also contains other trace minerals such as iron, potassium, phosphorus, selenium, and vitamin B_6. All good for you!

Always Toast Your Spices

There are probably places in this book where you can cut corners. I'm pretty down with improvising and being flexible with recipes. But one step I don't want you to skip is toasting spices—and this goes for BOTH whole and ground spices. I don't mean to be difficult, but I have to insist. Here's why.

Toasting your spices is critical to getting maximum flavor from the ingredient. All spices have essential oils tucked inside them, and to release them they have to be activated with heat. When you warm those spices and start to toast them, that's when those oils get released and the aroma and flavor come alive. If you want your spices to reach their full potential, this is an essential step.

Also, a note here that fresh spices really make a difference. I recently got back from India and brought a bunch of spices back and I forgot just how ridiculously fresh they are there and how decisive, potent, and flavorful they can be. It makes such a difference. Try to get your spices from a spice store if you can, a place like Kalustyan's or Sahadi if you live in the New York City area. Otherwise, as a general rule, whole spices will stay fresh for about 4 years, ground spices for 3 to 4 years, and dried leafy herbs for 1 to 3 years. If you can't remember the last time you bought a fresh jar of oregano, it may be time to get a new one!

While the toasting rule applies to both whole and ground spices, you should toast them in separate pans. Use a nonreactive sauté pan that conducts heat evenly, such as stainless steel or heavy cast iron, to ensure even roasting. Heat up the pan over medium heat, about the level you might use to fry eggs. Add the spices, and once the spices warm up, after 2 to 3 minutes (sooner for ground spices than whole), you will start smelling them. That's where you have to make sure to keep moving them in the pan constantly for about 45 seconds more so that the spices don't burn. Once the spices are very aromatic, you're done. Get them off the heat.

With ground spices, you can even take the pan off the heat once they start to smell and just keep pushing the spices around the pan to make sure they toast up evenly; the latent heat should be enough to do the trick. Whatever you do, make sure there's no smoking going on; if that happens, dump what's in the pan and start over using slightly more gentle heat.

Alternatively, you can toast spices in the oven. This is convenient if you already need to have the oven on for the rest of the recipe. Use an oven preheated to 350°F [180°C] and stir the spices around on a cookie sheet once in a while, as the edges may burn. The spices should be toasted within 5 to 8 minutes.

Either way, be sure to let your spices cool completely on a plate before grinding. You don't want to grind them while they're still hot because the essential oils are more active and the nature of grinding brings out heat. It will force the spices into a paste rather than a powder, which is not what you're looking for. We want powder, so let them cool.

Hemp Hearts

Hemp hearts, the edible interiors of the seed that hemp grows from, are a fantastic superfood that you'll probably start hearing about really soon, if you haven't already. Hemp hearts are a noticeable source of fiber and protein, are packed with vitamins, and are loaded up with calcium and iron. I like to sprinkle them on salads, blend them into smoothies, pop them on granola, and incorporate them into soups like the Tomato Soup with Spanish Lentils and Raisins (page 100), and the Creamy Broccoli and Coconut Soup (page 97) to add richness and protein. They would also be great as a garnish on the Acai Bowl with Fruit and Paleo Granola (page 59) for added plant protein.

What's a Soubise?

If you've never heard the word *soubise*, don't worry. You're not alone. Most people haven't; that's because it's one of those very classic French sauces that's taught only in French kitchens; I'm not even sure it's taught in culinary school. I learned it at La Folie in San Francisco cooking for Roland Passot.

It's super traditional, and oftentimes traditional things turn out to be quite useful and that's the case here. A soubise is made from thinly sliced onions cooked very slowly in lots of butter until the onions become soft and almost melt. They're then puréed into a sauce that's used for very rich meats such as veal cheeks or quail stuffed with foie gras. Did I mention it's really rich?

When I was cooking with Tom Colicchio at Gramercy Tavern, where I learned so much, Tom did a modified version with butter and onions but he added a teaspoon of Arborio rice. The rice starch gave it lots of richness and allowed him to use a bit less butter. That technique stayed with me.

At Indie Fresh, I developed a vegan soubise that I relied upon to make soups taste really creamy. Instead of sautéing the onions, I steamed them for about twenty minutes so they got super sweet and soft, then added coriander seed, Arborio rice (thanks, Tom), and almond milk, which mimics the butter. You'll find it makes soups taste as though you've poured in 1 pint [480 ml] of cream when you've added none. You'll find this recipe used in the Creamy Broccoli and Coconut Soup (page 97), Tomato Soup with Spanish Lentils and Raisins (page 100), and Smoked Fish Chowder (page 107). Pretty cool.

Vegan Soubise ^{GF DF V}

This vegan soubise is going to quickly become a kitchen standard you reach for again and again. That's because it makes soups taste like they are full of butter and cream, without any of the added fat. You're welcome!

MAKES 3 CUPS [680 G]

2 medium white or yellow onions, thinly sliced

½ tsp coriander seeds

½ tsp Arborio rice

3½ cups [840 ml] almond milk

First, place the onions in a steamer basket over about 3 in [7.5 cm] of boiling water for 12 to 15 minutes or until completely tender.

While the onions are steaming, toast the coriander seeds and Arborio rice in a small, dry pan (no oil) over medium heat for 4 to 5 minutes or until fragrant and lightly browned.

Next, spoon the soft, steamed onions into a medium saucepan over medium heat and pour the almond milk over the top to cover. Sprinkle in the toasted coriander and Arborio rice. Let it all simmer together and cook down by a quarter. This should take about 15 minutes.

Let cool slightly. When it's just warm, transfer to a blender and purée for 3 to 4 minutes, scraping down the sides of the blender several times to make sure all the ingredients get fully incorporated.

Store leftovers in an airtight container in the refrigerator for up to 1 week, or pour the soubise into an ice cube tray and take out cubes of it as needed. Frozen soubise cubes will last in the freezer for up to 3 months.

Ghee

Ghee, the rich, golden, clarified butter that is a staple of Indian cooking, was an essential food from my childhood; there was always a jar in the refrigerator. Ghee has since become a global phenomenon, trending as a superfood and beloved by followers of the popular keto diet, but I don't believe in eating that much fat. For regular cooking, I prefer to use olive oil or coconut oil. But I do cook with ghee on occasion, and when I do, I always make it from grass-fed cultured butter. Grass-fed butter makes an impact on the flavor; it gives the ghee a grassy, almost ripe-cheese taste. It helps to achieve more character.

MAKES 2 CUPS [440 G]

1 lb [455 g] unsalted grass-fed cultured butter

To make the ghee, melt the butter in a small pot over low heat. After 5 to 6 minutes, you will notice white foam coming to the surface as the butter simmers. Gently skim the foam away, being careful not to skim too much of the clear butter with it. You don't have to get all of the foam, as it will eventually sink to the bottom of the pot.

Let the butter simmer gently for another 10 minutes, letting the milk solids at the bottom of the pot settle and turn a golden brown. At this point, the simmering should be slowing down. Skim again; the liquid that is left should be mostly clear. It should smell very nutty.

After about another 5 minutes, when the butter is not simmering at all, strain it through doubled-up cheesecloth (a coffee filter works, too). This will leave you with a clear, golden-colored butter.

Store leftovers in an airtight container in the refrigerator; it lasts for 2 months.

Koji Butter GF VG

Koji, which is available on Amazon and in Asian grocery stores, is an enzyme used to make soy sauce and sake. A lot of chefs use it to rub on meat because it speeds up the aging process and tenderizes the meat. I prefer to use it to start a fermentation, which is how I make this butter. We add the koji to yogurt with live cultures and some heavy cream and let it ferment for 3 days out on the counter. By then it will look thick and creamy and can be transferred to the refrigerator to chill. Once you start to mix it, it will separate into solids and whey—butter and buttermilk, which I use to make pancakes at Alta Calidad. The butter is great with the Gluten-Free Bread (page 46) and on Grilled Corn with Koji Butter (page 157), but you could also flavor it: Add seaweed, sea salt, whatever you like. This is not a "light" butter; this is real full-fat butter. This isn't something you should be spreading on biscuits every day, but I am a believer that fat is not the enemy. Excess is. It's all about balance. The koji butter keeps for 3 to 5 days, but you must get all of the whey out of it, otherwise it will start to turn. You will know.

MAKES 2 CUPS [440 G]

1 qt [960 ml] heavy cream

2 Tbsp koji

1 tsp plain yogurt

First, combine all the ingredients in a small bowl, cover with plastic wrap, and poke a couple of holes in the plastic with the tip of a sharp paring knife. Leave the bowl out on the counter for 2 to 3 days in a shaded, cool area. After 2 to 3 days, it should be thick and set. Place the bowl in the refrigerator with the same plastic cover with the holes in it until it is chilled, about an hour.

Once the butter has rested for an hour in the refrigerator, transfer it to the bowl of a stand mixer (or a bowl to use a hand mixer). Using the whisk attachment, mix on medium speed until the mixture starts to separate, 5 to 8 minutes. Pour through a chinois or fine-mesh strainer to separate the whey from the solids. Scoop the solids back into a bowl and place covered in the refrigerator for about an hour to firm up. You can use the liquid part as buttermilk for pancakes, or discard it.

Once the solids are firm, wrap the butter in a large piece of cheesecloth and run it under cold water while softly squeezing the chilled butter until the water runs clear. Do this the same way you might mold clay, just so the butter gets clean. It should take about 5 minutes. Add the cleaned butter back to the bowl of the stand mixer and this time use the paddle attachment to mix on medium speed until the butter is creamed and looks like butter. This should take another 5 minutes.

Wrap the butter in plastic. Store leftovers in an airtight container in the refrigerator for 3 to 5 days.

Tomato Paste GF DF V

Tomato paste might sound like the most innocuous ingredient, and something you would never think twice about. But commercial brands of tomato paste are loaded with sugar. I'd rather not feed myself, my customers, and my family the unneeded extra sugar, so I found a way to make a paste that dramatically cuts down on the sugar content. Rather than refined sugars, I add whole fiber sugars from dates that your body has to work to process.

MAKES 1¼ CUPS [283 G]

¼ cup plus 1 tsp [65 ml] extra-virgin olive oil

½ small Spanish onion, sliced

5 medium garlic cloves, sliced

7 dates, pitted

7 plum tomatoes, seeded, roughly chopped, and puréed in the blender

1 tsp kosher salt

Heat the olive oil in a medium pot over low to medium heat, then add the onion and garlic. Sweat them for 8 to 10 minutes, until soft. Turn the heat to low, add the dates and puréed tomatoes, and cook until soft and the liquid is cooked out, about 1 hour. Cool for 5 to 10 minutes before transferring the contents of the pot to a blender. Purée for 3 to 4 minutes, scraping down the sides of the blender several times to make sure all the ingredients get fully incorporated. Season with the salt.

Store leftovers in an airtight container in the refrigerator for up to 1 week, or freeze in a zip-top bag or an ice cube tray for up to 3 months.

Romesco Sauce ^{GF DF V}

This is a traditional sauce found in Basque cooking where it's their most popular condiment. You'll find it slathered on grilled fish, toasted bread, and most famously at the annual festival of the Calçots, where towns-people celebrate the arrival of spring onions by grilling them over an open flame until they're charred. (Anthony Bourdain was a fan.) Made from olive oil, crushed nuts, roasted peppers, and a smoky pepper called pimenton, the sauce is versatile and vegan and marries well with really almost anything that needs a flash of flavor. It's the secret ingredient in my Gaz-pacho with Poached Shrimp (page 108), but you should try it on roasted vegetables, sand-wiches, and my bison burger (see page 86). We use piquillo peppers in this recipe because they are so sweet, but you can substitute roasted red peppers if you like.

MAKES 3 CUPS [680 G]

¾ cup [180 ml] extra-virgin olive oil

5 medium garlic cloves, thinly sliced

5 large shallots, thinly sliced

2 large carrots, peeled and thinly sliced into disks

2 medium piquillo peppers, seeds and centers removed, thinly sliced

1 large celery stalk, thinly sliced

1 Tbsp plus 2 tsp pimenton

Kosher salt

Heat the olive oil in a medium to large pot over medium heat. Add the garlic, shallots, carrots, piquillo peppers, and celery. Lower the heat to medium-low, stir, and cook until all the ingredients are soft, 20 to 25 minutes. Stir often to avoid burning. Sprinkle in and stir the pimenton, and take the pot off the heat. Let it cool for 5 to 10 minutes, then transfer the sauce to a blender and purée for 2 to 3 minutes, scraping down the sides of the blender several times to make sure all the ingredients get fully incor-porated. Season with salt.

Store leftovers in an airtight container in the refrigerator for up to 1 week, or in the freezer for up to 3 months.

Basic Homemade Mayo

Fresh homemade mayo is really nice to have on hand for all of the aiolis in this book. It's a simple recipe, and it makes dressings taste that much better because it's from scratch. Mine is even healthier than the average mayo because it's made with egg yolks, olive oil, avocado oil, and lemon. That said, vegan mayo—often called fabanaise, which is made from chickpea water—is a very good substitute. It's delicious and easy to find. Feel free to use a fabanaise of your choice when Basic Homemade Mayo is called for in any recipes.

MAKES ¾ CUP [180 G]

2 egg yolks

¾ cup [180 ml] mixed oil (half extra-virgin olive oil and half avocado oil)

¼ tsp fresh lemon juice

¼ tsp kosher salt, or more as needed

Place the egg yolks in a medium bowl. With the oils in a single measuring cup, whisk the yolks and slowly add the oil in a thin stream. Continue whisking as you do this. Add the lemon juice, 1 Tbsp of water, and the salt. Continue whisking until the ingredients are incorporated and reach a mayonnaise-like consistency. It should need to be whisked for less than a minute more after you add the lemon juice and water. The oil and egg will bring it to the right consistency. It does not need to chill before being used.

Store leftovers in an airtight container in the refrigerator for 3 to 5 days.

Mojo de Ajo GF DF V

Mojo de ajo is a traditional garlic bath, similar to Italy's *bagna càuda*. It's made from lots of minced fresh garlic, lime juice, and ground chile piquin, a specific chile powder that is extremely hot. It makes everything addictive. In this recipe, I use Tajín, which is made of dried limes and dried red chiles. You can find it near the spice section in most grocery stores or order it online. You can drizzle this sauce over sautéed shrimp or try it on my Roast Lamb Shoulder with Olive Veracruzana (page 146).

MAKES 1 CUP [226 G]

15 to 18 garlic cloves (1½ to 2 heads), peeled

¾ cups [180 ml] extra-virgin olive oil

Juice of ½ medium orange

Juice of 1 lime

2 tsp tamari

¼ tsp Tajín seasoning

First, process the garlic cloves in your food processor until they are finely minced, but not a paste. You will need to scrape the sides of the bowl and mix the garlic up a few times to achieve evenly minced garlic.

Next, heat the oil in a medium saucepan over medium-low heat. Add the minced garlic and cook for 5 to 7 minutes, being careful not to burn the garlic. Stir it often and adjust the heat as necessary to keep the oil and garlic lightly simmering.

Add the orange juice, lime juice, and tamari. Simmer for another 6 to 7 minutes, until it is a light golden color.

Finally, add the Tajín and cook for 7 to 8 minutes, watching carefully so the garlic doesn't burn. It will turn a nice golden color from the heat and the tamari.

Remove the pan from the heat and let the mixture cool for 15 minutes. Store in an airtight container in the refrigerator. Mojo de ajo will last up to 1 month in the refrigerator but doesn't freeze well.

Acai Purée GF DF V

The acai berry is a 1 in [2.5 cm] long, reddish-purple fruit that comes from the acai palm tree, which is native to the Amazon. Its nutrient-dense pulp is rich in antioxidants, may fight cancer, lowers cholesterol, and boosts brain function. It's not surprising that the acai berry has become a trendy superfood to toss into smoothies and fruit bowls. Acai comes in a frozen juice and you can find it sweetened or unsweetened; I use the unsweetened juice. I blend the juice with fresh bananas and almond milk, and that becomes a good-for-you base for fresh fruit or granola. It makes a great vinaigrette because it has a lot of acidity; you could also marinate proteins in it.

MAKES 1¼ CUPS [283 G]

2 medium ripe bananas
½ cup [120 ml] acai juice
3 Tbsp vegan protein powder
1½ Tbsp almond milk

Add all the ingredients to the blender and purée for 3 to 4 minutes, scraping down the sides of the blender several times to make sure all the ingredients get fully incorporated. It should be a pudding-like consistency. Store leftovers in an airtight container in the refrigerator for 1 to 2 days.

Cashew Purée GF DF V

Think of this cashew purée as a revolutionary béchamel sauce—it adds richness with a plant-based non-dairy fat. It does take a little bit of time and effort to make because the cashews have to be soaked, boiled, and strained, but the texture benefits make it worth the time commitment. You'll find it all over this book, in the Chicken and Black Bean Chili (page 110) and Creamy Broccoli and Coconut Soup (page 97) as well as the Turkey Lasagna (page 138) and Bison Meatballs with Cremini Mushroom Sauce and Quinoa (page 143). I like to make this in advance for the week, and keep it in the refrigerator so it's on hand.

MAKES 1½ CUPS [340 G]

10½ oz [300 g] raw cashews

2 Tbsp plus 1 tsp extra-virgin olive oil

¼ tsp grated nutmeg

⅛ tsp kosher salt

First, soak the cashews in ¼ cup plus 2 Tbsp [90 ml] of room-temperature water for 2 hours, making sure all the cashews are fully submerged in the water.

Next, drain the cashews, discarding the liquid. Spoon the soaked cashews into a blender with ¼ cup [60 ml] of water, the olive oil, nutmeg, and salt, and purée for 3 to 4 minutes, scraping down the sides of the blender several times to make sure all the ingredients get fully incorporated. You may need to add an extra drop or two of water to bring it together.

Store leftovers in an airtight container in the refrigerator for 5 to 7 days.

The Best Basic Marinade GF DF VG

I use this marinade all the time—on fish and meat, even on hearty vegetables like Brussels sprouts. I like how herbaceous it is, and the honey, tamari, and ginger help any protein caramelize beautifully. To avoid any prolonged temperature fluctuations which could cause food-borne illness, when you marinate, do it in the refrigerator. I suggest a minimum of 30 minutes and up to 4 hours.

MAKES 3 CUPS [720 ML]

24 garlic cloves, sliced (about 2 heads)

Juice of 2 medium oranges

½ bunch cilantro, including stems

2¼ cup [45 g] baby arugula or watercress, tightly packed

1½ cups [360 ml] extra-virgin olive oil

2 in [5 cm] piece fresh ginger, peeled and sliced into thin coins

2 tsp honey

1 Tbsp tamari

Place all the ingredients in a blender and purée for 3 to 4 minutes, scraping down the sides of the blender several times to make sure all the ingredients get fully incorporated. Store leftovers in an airtight container in the refrigerator for up to a week or freeze for up to 3 months.

My Mexican Marinade

This is one of my favorite marinades for whole chickens because it gets the skin super crispy, almost like a potato chip, which is amazing when you think about it. A roast chicken wrapped up in a potato chip? That's nice. (The recipe is on page 134.) Here's a tip: After you're done marinating, let your chicken sit out on the counter to come up close to room temperature before you roast it. Cold meat takes longer to heat in the oven, so this way the meat cooks faster and more evenly. It's a little step but it makes a difference.

MAKES 1 CUP [240 ML]

5 guajillo chiles

¼ cup [60 ml] extra-virgin olive oil

¼ cup [60 ml] fresh lime juice

¼ cup [35 g] raisins

3 medium garlic cloves, peeled

2 Tbsp tamari

2 Tbsp dried oregano, preferably Mexican

1 Tbsp freshly ground black pepper, toasted

1 tsp red pepper flakes

Seed and soak the guajillo chiles in hot water for 10 to 15 minutes, until soft. Drain and place in a blender.

Place the rest of the ingredients in the blender and purée for 3 to 4 minutes, scraping down the sides of the blender several times to make sure all the ingredients get fully incorporated. This will give you about 1 cup [240 ml] of marinade.

Store leftovers in an airtight container in the refrigerator for up to 1 week or freeze for up to 3 months.

GOOD TO KNOW: Marinades and Brines

Each does its own thing. Marinades impart flavor; brines add moisture. Marinades tend to be sauces made from a mix of acid, salt, fruit or vegetables, and spices. But marinades don't really penetrate the whole protein. Brines—which can be wet or dry—do. A dry brine is sort of like the pre-salting you might do to a beef jerky; the salt-based spice paste is left on for a long period of time to penetrate the meat. A wet brine also uses salt but in combination with water and some aromatics. Just remember: Discard marinades and brines after using them once. They cannot safely be used again.

GOOD TO KNOW: My Brine

The brine I use at Alta Calidad is Mexican-ish. I start out with two parts salt to one-quarter part agave, which has a less direct sweetness than cane sugar, and then add Mexican oregano and chipotle in adobo. Let your chicken bathe in that liquid for any amount of time. Even if it's just 10 minutes, it's better than nothing.

Once you've brined the chicken, take it out and pat it dry. You could roast it as is, but I like to massage a marinade made with tamari, raisins, chiles, and lime juice into the skin to give it a gorgeous crackling texture.

Basic Quinoa GF DF V

Quinoa is a super superfood. It is gluten free and a complete protein (meaning it contains all nine essential amino acids) and is an excellent source of fiber, protein, B vitamins, and iron. It's easy to make, and adds nutrition and texture to nearly anything. It's only downside is that it's a bit bland, so I tend to pair it with recipes that have a lot of flavor. I use it in the Yuba Noodle Salad with Ginger Dressing and Raw Vegetables (page 81), the Black Bean and Sweet Potato Burger with Truffled Mayo (page 88), the Moroccan Carrot Soup (page 99), and the Bison Meatballs with Cremini Mushroom Sauce (page 143). You can also toss it in salads and serve it instead of rice with chicken or fish.

MAKES 2½ CUPS [300 G]

1 cup [180 g] quinoa
1½ Tbsp kosher salt

Bring the quinoa, salt, and 8 cups [2 L] of water to a boil. Lower the heat slightly so it's still between a boil and a simmer.

Cook for 10 to 15 minutes, until the grains are tender but have a little pop to them; you will see some of the seeds starting to sprout a bit. Drain the quinoa. Store in an airtight container in the refrigerator for up to 5 days.

Gluten-Free Pasta GF DF VG

This recipe makes enough pasta for my Turkey Lasagna (page 138) and is generally best for baked dishes. You'll need a lot of egg yolks for this recipe, which help keep the texture as light as possible. Gluten-free flour makes a much more brittle and crumbly pasta than traditional all-purpose flour. While you can put traditional pasta dough through a pasta machine a few times, you can't with this dough—it will disintegrate. So as soon as you get it to the desired thickness, you're done.

MAKES 2½ LB [1.2 KG]

4½ cups [560 g or 20 oz] gluten-free flour

1 Tbsp extra-virgin olive oil

1 Tbsp almond milk

2 egg yolks

3 whole eggs

1 Tbsp Cashew Purée (page 37)

First, pour the flour in the bowl of a stand mixer fitted with the hook attachment and start mixing on low speed. Drizzle in the olive oil and almond milk (alternate the two) and mix for 30 seconds or until just incorporated.

Add the yolks one at a time, waiting until each is mostly incorporated before adding the next. Then add the whole eggs, one at a time.

Scrape down the sides of the bowl when necessary during this process to ensure every ingredient is getting evenly mixed.

Add the cashew purée and mix for 3 to 4 minutes, until the dough is smooth. Gather the dough on a clean surface and form it into a disk shape, then wrap it tightly with plastic wrap. Store it in the refrigerator for 3 to 5 days.

Gluten-Free Roti GF DF V

I came up with the idea of using roti at Alta Calidad as a way to expand the concept of a tortilla. It marries my Indian culture with my Mexican kitchen. This roti is made from vegan butter, chia seeds, and a little masa (or Maseca, which is like a corn flour, found in most any grocery store, if you don't have fresh masa). Once the dough is formed, cook it on a skillet or a griddle like you would a tortilla. Large roti can be treated like a burrito wrapper, or served with Black Lentils (page 164). Done smaller, it's terrific for quesadillas for kids. The roti are also delicious when served warmed up with some Ghee (page 27).

MAKES 4 ROTI

½ cup [113 g] packed raw masa or Maseca

¼ cup plus 2 tsp [39 g] tapioca starch

¼ cup [32 g or 1 oz] coconut flour

2 tsp vegan butter

1¾ tsp chia seeds

1¼ tsp flaxseed

1 tsp canola oil, plus more for cooking

½ tsp kosher salt

¼ cup [60 ml] boiling water

TO MAKE THE DOUGH: First, add all the ingredients, except the boiling water, to the bowl of a stand mixer fitted with the paddle attachment. Mix on low speed to incorporate everything, for about 1 minute.

Next, slowly add the boiling water in a stream until a dough begins to form. Mix on medium speed for about 10 minutes until the dough is smooth to the touch.

On a clean surface or a dish towel, divide the dough into four equal balls and keep them covered with a damp cloth. The dough works much better when it's cold, so refrigerate it for about 15 minutes before you start to roll it out. Once the dough has had time to chill, put a dough ball between two pieces of parchment paper and roll it out until it is about ⅛ in [4 mm] thick or about 6 in [15 cm] in diameter. Repeat with the remaining dough balls.

Spray both sides of each dough disk with cooking spray and keep them in the refrigerator between the pieces of parchment paper until ready to use. Roti dough can be cooked immediately or tightly wrapped in plastic wrap and stored in the refrigerator for 1 to 2 days.

TO MAKE THE ROTI: Heat about 1 tsp of canola oil in a heavy-bottomed pan (cast iron works well here) over low to medium heat. Make sure the pan is large enough for one 6 in [15 cm] roti. Peel off one piece of parchment and place the roti on the pan, then peel off the parchment from the other side. Cook for 45 seconds to 1 minute on each side. You will know that the roti is done when it turns from translucent to a more opaque color. Think of this like you would cooking pancakes: The first batch takes a little longer and then, as the pan heats more, it goes faster, so you may want to lower the heat as you cook. Repeat with the remaining dough.

Keep the cooked roti wrapped in parchment paper with olive oil brushed on each side so they don't stick. Store leftovers in an airtight container in the refrigerator for 5 to 7 days.

Gluten-Free Bread GF V

This is a great bread, but it's not a sandwich bread. It's a nice loaf for people who cannot tolerate gluten, but it's best sliced thickly, toasted, and topped with butter or eggs. I make it with almond flour, baking soda, yogurt, and vinegar to help soften the bread and inflate it so that it's less dense than your average gluten-free bread. Slather slices of this bread with grass-fed butter, nut butter, or dunk a slice in the Tomato Soup with Spanish Lentils and Raisins (page 100).

MAKES 1 LOAF (FOR A 5 BY 9 IN [12 BY 23 CM] STANDARD LOAF PAN)

2 cups plus 3 Tbsp [270 g or 7¼ oz] almond flour

⅔ cup plus 4 tsp [93 g] tapioca starch

⅔ cup [60 g] ground flaxseed

2 tsp kosher salt

1 tsp baking soda

6 eggs

½ cup [120 g] full-fat Greek yogurt

1 Tbsp agave

¾ cup [180 ml] extra-virgin olive oil

1½ tsp cider vinegar

Preheat the oven to 350°F [180°C].

First, add the almond flour, tapioca starch, ground flaxseed, salt, and baking soda to the bowl of a stand mixer fitted with the paddle attachment and set aside. Next, in a medium bowl, lightly whisk together the eggs, yogurt, and agave (it doesn't have to be smooth, just mixed enough so it can pour into the larger bowl easily). With the mixer on low, mix the dry ingredients until they are incorporated, about 1 minute. Add one-third of the olive oil, mix for 30 seconds, then add half of the wet ingredients, mixing for another 30 seconds.

Continue to alternate the olive oil and the wet ingredients, starting and ending with the olive oil. Add the vinegar and mix for 45 seconds to 1 minute, scraping the sides and bottom of the bowl with a spatula to make sure all the ingredients are incorporated. It's a thick, but wet, dough. It won't easily pour into the loaf pan; you will have to scoop it in.

Spray the loaf pan with cooking spray so it's evenly coated and scoop the dough into the pan. You can wet your hands and use them to gently push the dough into the pan and smooth the top.

Bake on the middle rack of the oven for 1 hour, or until a cake tester comes out clean when inserted in the very middle of the loaf. Let cool for 5 to 10 minutes before taking the loaf out of the pan and cooling the rest of the way on a wire rack. Store leftovers, wrapped tightly in plastic, in the refrigerator for 3 to 5 days.

CHAPTER TWO

GOOD

BREAKI

GOOD

MORNI

FAST,

NG

While most families eat dinner together, as a chef that's harder for me to do. Breakfast tends to be the meal that Ela and I can always have together, which is super important to me. The most meaningful thing I've ever done in my life is being her dad.

When she was two, her mom and I split up and I became a single parent. My former wife, Heidi, has helped make it as seamless as possible. I'm still close with her; we are good friends and we work very well together as co-parents. That said, being a single dad and a chef is tough. I know you've heard that from moms, and as a dad, I'll second that. It's really hard. It took me a while to figure out how to do both, because I knew I wanted to really be in Ela's life, not just someone who came by to celebrate her birthday or drop in on occasion.

At first, I really didn't know how to make it work. When Ela was born, I was in the process of opening my first solo restaurant, the modern Indian restaurant Elettaria, and my attention wasn't on diapers and feedings; it was on developing dynamic menus and working food costs.

I was heartbroken when Elettaria closed, and in the process, I lost a lot. My marriage fell apart, my career was on the rocks, and I was broke. It was very difficult time in my life. It took me about six months to find a path out of that darkness after the restaurant closed. I spent a lot of time with Ela and slowly I began to understand. It was really then that I associated my life with being a parent first. Ela and I were getting closer and I started feeling better.

So, instead of going back to being a traditional chef, I found consulting gigs, helping other chefs open and scale their own concepts, not mine. I made a plan with Heidi for shared custody. And I built a work life that is incredibly busy and rewarding, but that also allows me to have Ela at my house during the week and on weekends, to take her to school, to pick her up from dance class, and to take her on vacations with me where I can really get that quality time and also share some of my favorite food cities with her.

Since breakfast is a time we are often together, I tend to make more elaborate meals; there's rarely cold cereal. She loves the Pumpkin Protein Pancakes (page 66), the Weekend Waffles (page 68), the Acai Bowl with Fruit and Paleo Granola (page 59), and every smoothie in this chapter. The one thing Ela doesn't like is eggs. I don't understand how this is possible given how much I love them, but I guess at some point we have to realize our kids aren't our clones. Thankfully.

Blueberry Ginger Smoothie <small>GF DF V</small>

Blueberries are antioxidant powerhouses and ginger is an anti-inflammatory root that has many medicinal uses, from helping fight colds to aiding in digestion. These two ingredients together in a morning smoothie makes a lot of sense, especially if you're starting to feel run down. This recipe calls for frozen bananas, but if you don't have a frozen banana on hand, you can just use a regular banana with two ice cubes and that will work just fine. The almond butter should be unsweetened and unsalted.

SERVES 2

¾ cup [105 g] fresh or frozen blueberries

½ cup [120 ml] coconut water

¼ cup [60 ml] almond milk

¼ cup [65 g] almond butter (unsweetened, unsalted, and roasted)

1 small frozen banana

¼ in [6 mm] piece fresh ginger, peeled and minced

1 tsp maple syrup

¼ tsp ground cinnamon

Combine all the ingredients in a blender and purée for 3 to 4 minutes, scraping down the sides of the blender several times to make sure all the ingredients get fully incorporated. Serve immediately.

GOOD TO KNOW:
Smoothies

Everyone tells you to eat breakfast. And I know this book is supposed to be about good food and healthy habits, but in this case, I'm just going to come clean. I am guilty of not eating breakfast and of drinking way too much coffee. That's not to say I don't like breakfast—I love breakfast foods, especially eggs, but by the time I get around to eating breakfast it's already lunchtime. And not because I'm in bed sleeping off the night before; those days are long gone. I'm one of those annoying people who works out every morning and I tend to eat after I work out. Once I am back from the gym—these days I am into boxing and these high-intensity interval training workouts—I usually have one of these smoothies.

It's sort of a mistaken belief that fruit is the only thing you can put in smoothies. Sure, you can make them with almost all fruit, sort of like a milkshake, but when I'm making them for myself, I tend to like them to be a little less sweet and more like a meal. I always add a vegan protein powder because it has a neutral flavor so that the other ingredients can shine. I also prefer to use fruit that's high in sugar rather than add refined sugar, so something like dates or bananas adds a good amount of sweetness with fiber and nutrients. Rather than make the smoothies with dairy, which upsets my stomach, I use almond milk and sometimes coconut water, but you can use milk if you prefer that, with equal substitutions. Have a great morning!

Avocado, Mango, and Coconut Smoothie _{GF DF V}

Avocados are all over my menu at Alta Calidad—on tacos, salads, and eggs, and, naturally, in bowls of fresh guacamole. Because they're packed with protein and nutrients and are the only fruit that contains heart-healthy monounsaturated fat, I like to start my day with avocados as often as possible. If you're used to reaching for fruit for your morning smoothie, it may seem strange to add an avocado, but trust me, they make smoothies rich and creamy. I tend to use frozen mango, just because it makes for a thicker smoothie. The coconut water and coconut milk add just the right amount of sweetness and nuttiness to make this a weekday favorite.

SERVES 2

1½ cup [30 g] packed spinach leaves

1 cup [240 ml] coconut water

1 cup [226 g] diced mango

⅓ cup [73 g] diced avocado (about half of a small avocado)

¼ cup [60 ml] coconut milk

½ tsp matcha powder

⅛ tsp kosher salt

Combine all the ingredients in a blender and purée for 3 to 4 minutes, scraping down the sides of the blender several times to make sure all the ingredients get fully incorporated. Serve immediately.

GOOD TO KNOW: Vegan Protein Powder

For anyone who is vegetarian or vegan, or even trying to just cut down on animal protein, protein powder is an easy way to replace that lost protein from your diet each day. I tend to reach for protein powder for all my morning smoothies. I also mix it into muffins and nut butters or even a bowl of oatmeal. I always choose a vegan protein powder, which really just means that the protein is coming from plants (think nuts, seeds, grains, and legumes) rather than animal products (like dairy, meat, and eggs).

You can use any kind of vegan protein powder for the recipes in this book—soy, hemp, pea, rice, or peanut—but soy is the only complete vegan protein, containing all nine essential amino acids. In terms of brands, Aloha, Ladder, or Performix are brands I tend to like. So if you're not using a soy protein powder, look for a powder that combines protein sources, such as pea and rice. Make sure you read the label and that you can recognize the ingredients; you really don't want to eat anything you don't understand.

Almond Cacao Smoothie GF DF V

For this smoothie, I use cacao nibs. They're often called nature's chocolate chips, made from crushed cacao beans. They're super good for you, packed with powerful nutrients, antioxidants, and fiber. Nibs have an intense chocolatey taste, but aren't sweet at all. These little nuggets also boost your metabolism, so that's why I've put them in this morning smoothie. The bananas together with the almond milk make a smoothie that's rich and creamy and dairy free, too.

SERVES 2

1 cup plus 1 Tbsp [255 ml] almond milk

⅓ cup [80 ml] coconut water

¼ cup [65 g] almond butter (unsweetened, unsalted, and roasted)

¼ cup [56 g] Paleo Granola (facing page) or granola of your choice

2 dates, pitted

1 large frozen banana

1 Tbsp cocoa nibs

1 Tbsp vegan protein powder, (optional, see page 55)

Combine all the ingredients in a blender and purée for 3 to 4 minutes, scraping down the sides of the blender several times to make sure all the ingredients get fully incorporated. Serve immediately.

Paleo Granola with Cashews, Pecans, Almonds, and Figs GF DF V

If you like to start your day with granola and yogurt, this is going to be your new go-to recipe. I love the combination of toasted nuts and seeds with coconut and fig purée. It's gluten free and will give you lots of energy whenever you need it. If you tend to snack, stash a jar in your office for when your stomach starts to grumble. You can make this in advance and keep it in an airtight jar for weeks (though it will probably be eaten sooner than that!). One more thing: I like to use a fig purée for sweetness in this recipe but you can substitute unsweetened applesauce if you don't want to bother making it.

SERVES 4 TO 6

1⅓ cups [160 g] raw pecans

1 cup [140 g] raw cashews

2 cups [280 g] raw almonds (whole, slivered, or sliced)

2 cups [160 g] shredded unsweetened coconut

¾ cup [105 g] pumpkin seeds

¼ cup [56 g] Fig Purée (page 174) or unsweetened applesauce

¾ tsp kosher salt

Preheat the oven to 200°F [95°C].

Line an 8 by 16 in [20 by 40.5 cm] sheet tray with parchment paper and set aside.

In the bowl of a food processor, pulse the pecans and cashews (and almonds, if using whole) 3 or 4 times, keeping the pieces fairly large. Pour the chopped nuts into a large bowl and add the almonds (if already slivered or sliced), coconut, pumpkin seeds, fig purée, and salt. Grab a sturdy wooden spoon and mix well.

Transfer the mixture to the prepared sheet tray and spread it out evenly.

Bake the granola for 40 to 45 minutes, stirring it with a spoon 2 or 3 times while baking, until golden brown and crunchy. Store leftovers in an airtight container at room temperature for a couple of weeks.

Acai Bowl with Fruit and Paleo Granola GF DF V

You've seen acai bowls all over town, but the ones sold in cafes are packed with fruit and sugar-heavy granola. Instead, this one stays clean; my acai is made with bananas and protein powder. I like to top it with strawberries, fresh bananas, and blueberries, but feel free to go for whatever fruit is in season. Apples are great in the fall, and if you like passion fruit, that's delicious on here, too. I let the acai set in the refrigerator before topping with fresh sliced fruit and my Paleo Granola.

SERVES 4

2 cups [453 g] Acai Purée (page 36)

1 cup [226 g] Paleo Granola (page 57)

Sliced fresh fruit (such as strawberries, bananas, and blueberries) and dried coconut, for garnish

Divide the acai purée evenly between four bowls. Divide the granola evenly and sprinkle it on top of each bowl of acai and garnish generously with fresh fruit and shredded coconut.

Gluten-Free Steel-Cut Oatmeal with Chia Seeds GF DF V

This oatmeal is a warm and wonderful way to get your day started. I use gluten-free oats for this recipe, but you can use regular oats if you prefer. The chia seeds add protein and act as a thickener, making the oatmeal rich and creamy. I cook the oatmeal in almond milk and water and then sprinkle it with chia seeds. Feel free to add any berries you like; I like the brightness of goji berries, myself. You can also add some butter to melt over the top, or make it savory and top it with a sunny-side-up egg, kind of like risotto.

SERVES 4 TO 6

1 Tbsp coconut oil

1¼ cups [200 g] gluten-free steel-cut oats

3 Tbsp pumpkin seeds

1½ Tbsp flaxseed

2 tsp hemp hearts

1½ tsp chia seeds

¼ cup [56 g] unsweetened pumpkin purée

1 tsp kosher salt

¼ cup [56 g] Cashew Purée (page 37)

Sliced fresh fruit and chopped nuts, for garnish

Melt the coconut oil in a large pot over medium heat. Add the oats, pumpkin seeds, flaxseed, hemp hearts, and chia seeds. Stir continuously and toast until nutty and fragrant, 6 to 8 minutes. The pumpkin seeds should begin to puff up and the oats will look more golden in color.

Add 3½ cups [840 ml] of water, the pumpkin purée, and the salt. Bring to a simmer and stir often. It should be looking creamy and have some liquid left in it.

When the oats are halfway cooked, after 12 to 15 minutes, stir in the cashew purée and cook for another 10 to 12 minutes, until fully cooked. Add more water if needed. The oats will still have a bite to them since they are steel cut.

Serve warm and top with fresh fruit and some chopped nuts, if you like. Store leftovers in an airtight container in the refrigerator for 3 to 5 days. Add a little water when reheating.

Morning Glory Muffins GF DF V

I don't really allow myself to eat muffins in the morning anymore; I'm more of a protein guy at my age. But these muffins are healthy enough that you can make them for yourself and the kids in the morning (or sneak them into a lunch box as a special treat).

I've made them vegan, and they have a gluten-free base, so that's a good start. Instead of butter or oil, I use apples and carrots in the batter, which give the muffins lots of moisture. This recipe calls for coconut sugar, but feel free to substitute dark brown sugar if you prefer. I think an apple with some tartness as well as sweetness is best for this recipe, so I've used Granny Smiths. Finally, this recipe takes a bit longer in the oven due to the chia seeds, so watch out for gooey centers. Be patient and give them enough time, about 30 minutes or until the cake tester comes out clean.

MAKES 12 MUFFINS

½ cup [226 g] vegan butter, plus more for coating the muffin tins

2 Tbsp chia seeds

1¼ cups [155 g or 5.5 oz] gluten-free flour

⅓ cup [40 g or 1.5 oz] almond flour

1 tsp baking soda

1 tsp baking powder

½ tsp ground cinnamon

½ tsp kosher salt

½ cup plus 1 Tbsp [128 g] coconut sugar

2 small carrots (or 1 medium), peeled and grated

1 medium apple, peeled and grated

½ medium zucchini, grated

¼ tsp vanilla extract

6 to 8 dates, pitted and coarsely chopped

½ cup [70 g] golden raisins

⅓ cup [45 g] pumpkin seeds, toasted and chopped

Preheat the oven to 350°F [180°C].

Evenly coat a standard muffin tin with vegan butter.

In a small bowl, mix the chia seeds with ¼ cup plus 1 Tbsp [75 ml] of water and let stand for at least 15 minutes, but no more than 1 hour, otherwise it will become sticky and gelatinous.

Meanwhile, in a medium bowl, mix the flours, baking soda, baking powder, cinnamon, and salt together with a whisk to break up any lumps in the flour and evenly incorporate the dry ingredients. Set aside.

Next, mix the sugar and butter in a stand mixer fitted with the paddle attachment on medium speed for 3 to 5 minutes, scraping down the bowl once or twice in the middle of mixing.

Add the chia seeds and mix for another 2 minutes.

Add the carrots, apple, zucchini (making sure all the liquid is squeezed out), and vanilla, and mix for 1 minute.

Slowly add the dry ingredients and gently mix for 1 minutes. Scrape the bowl to make sure it's evenly mixed. Fold in the chopped dates and raisins.

Fill the tins to the top and sprinkle the pumpkin seeds on top, pressing them gently down on the muffins.

Bake for 12 minutes, rotate the pan, and bake for another 12 to 15 minutes, or until the muffins are golden brown and a cake tester comes out clean when inserted in the center.

Store leftovers, wrapped in plastic, in the refrigerator for 3 to 5 days or freeze for up to 4 weeks.

Egg "Tostadas" GF DF VG

Breakfast tacos were my inspiration for these egg tostadas that I serve with a variety of condiments—you can go the Indian route with Coconut Chutney, bring in a little heat from Mexico with the Guajillo Salsa, or make them more refined with a Truffled Mayo.

SERVES 4

4 Gluten-Free Roti (page 45)

8 eggs, scrambled, fried, or sunny-side up

Coconut Chutney (page 216), for garnish

Guajillo Salsa (page 205), for garnish

Truffled Mayo (page 194), for garnish

Handful of chives, minced, for garnish

Handful of cilantro, chopped, for garnish

Cook the roti in a skillet over medium heat following the directions on page 45. You'll want to cook these a little longer to crisp them up, about 2 minutes on each side.

Prepare your eggs as you like them, scrambled, fried, or sunny-side up.

Divide the eggs on top of the roti and top with chutney, salsa, or mayo, and minced chives or chopped cilantro.

Poblano Shakshuka Eggs with Tomatoes, Cumin, and Harissa GF DF VG

I love eggs. They're my favorite food and I eat them all the time—the whole egg, not just the whites. Eggs are full of protein and good fats, and are quick to cook and eat any time of day. This egg dish is my Mexican variation on shakshuka—the spicy Israeli baked egg and tomato dish. I make it with a mixture of eggplant, tomatoes, and chiles and cook the eggs at the last moment so they're still soft and runny with a little sprinkle of sea salt to finish. Serve this with with Gluten-Free Bread (page 46), or your favorite country bread. I like this with a plain green salad dressed with the Lemony Vinaigrette (page 197).

SERVES 4

½ small eggplant, diced in ½ in [12 mm] cubes

1 or 2 tsp extra-virgin olive oil

2 Tbsp Mojo de Ajo (page 35)

½ small Spanish onion, diced

½ red bell pepper, diced

½ poblano pepper, diced

1½ tsp kosher salt

2 tsp ground cumin

2 tsp smoked paprika

2 small plum tomatoes, diced

4 eggs

Italian parsley, for garnish (optional)

Preheat the oven to 400°F [200°C]. Line an 8 by 16 in [20 by 40.5 cm] sheet tray with parchment paper.

Toss the diced eggplant with the olive oil. Spread the eggplant on the sheet tray and roast for 7 to 10 minutes or until halfway cooked.

Remove the sheet tray and set aside. Lower the oven to 300°F [150°C].

In a medium ovenproof skillet over low to medium heat, heat the mojo de ajo and add the onion, pepper, and poblano with ½ tsp of the salt. Cook for 10 minutes. Add the cumin and paprika and cook for another 2 minutes.

Add the tomatoes, the roasted eggplant, and another ½ tsp of the salt, stir together, cover with a lid, and put the skillet into the oven. Cook for 15 to 18 minutes until everything is very tender.

While it's cooking, separate the egg whites and yolks. The whites can be together in one bowl, but I find it helpful to keep the 4 yolks separate from each other (in small ramekins or small prep bowls) so they won't break as easily when you add them back in.

Remove the skillet from the oven, and over a very low heat, stir in a little egg white at a time, mixing well to ensure the white is cooked before adding more. Once the whites are incorporated and cooked into the vegetables, turn off the heat and use the back of your spoon to make four little "nests" for the yolks, placing them evenly around the skillet.

Pour the yolks (carefully, so they don't break) into the nests and cover the skillet to cook the yolks to your desired doneness. If you like them runny, this should only take 2 minutes. Garnish with Italian parsley, if desired. Serve immediately. Each serving should have a yolk when put on a plate.

Pumpkin Protein Pancakes GF DF VG

Pancakes are such a fun way to start the morning, and they're a breakfast my daughter loves. But given my propensity toward healthful meals, I felt I needed to transform the traditional pancake from something with nearly no nutritional value into something that's better for you (and your family). These have flaxseed (which are loaded with healthy fat, antioxidants, and fiber), and are gluten free. To make them even better for you, I've added unsweetened pumpkin purée (high in fiber, potassium, and vitamin C). I still flip them in a skillet the way I would ordinary pancakes, though I use coconut oil. You'll feel good knowing you're sending your kids out the door with a solid breakfast that will keep them satisfied until lunch. Or wrap them up and put them in their lunch boxes!

SERVES 4 TO 6

1 cup [156 g or 5½ oz] gluten-free flour (or 1 cup [120 g or 4¼ oz] sifted all-purpose flour if you prefer)

2¼ tsp baking powder

2 tsp ground flaxseed

¼ tsp baking soda

¼ tsp kosher salt

2 eggs

1½ cups [360 ml] coconut milk

¼ cup [56 g] unsweetened pumpkin purée

2½ tsp Cashew Purée (page 37)

1½ tsp cider vinegar

Maple syrup and sliced fresh fruit, for garnish

First, whisk together the flour, baking powder, flaxseed, baking soda, and salt in a small bowl.

Next, in a large bowl, whisk the eggs with the coconut milk, pumpkin purée, cashew purée, and vinegar.

Add the dry ingredients to the wet ingredients in the large bowl and whisk it all together.

Heat an electric griddle to 400°F [200°C], or set a stove-top griddle on medium heat. Or you could use a large nonstick pan as well. Just make sure it's pretty hot before cooking the pancakes. You may need to use some cooking spray to coat the pan or griddle.

Spoon a heaping spoonful of batter onto the hot surface. Let cook for 5 minutes, flip, and cook for another 5 minutes. Let the pancakes rest for at least 5 minutes before eating. Serve with maple syrup and fresh fruit. Store leftover pancakes, wrapped in plastic or foil, in the refrigerator for 2 to 3 days, or in the freezer for 4 to 6 weeks.

Weekend Waffles GF DF VG

These waffles are a wonderful way to start a weekend off right. They're hearty and nourishing and smell delicious while cooking. I like to top them with bananas, strawberries, and blueberries, but feel free to use whatever fruit you have on hand. Drizzle them with maple syrup or spoon over some of my Fig Purée (page 174).

SERVES 4 TO 6

One ¼ oz [7 g] packet dry active yeast

¼ cup [60 ml] warm water

1 Tbsp vegan butter

1⅓ cups [208 g or 7¼ oz] gluten-free flour

1 Tbsp coconut sugar

¾ tsp kosher salt

¼ tsp baking soda

2 eggs

1½ cups [360 ml] almond milk

Maple syrup, for serving

Fresh fruit, such as bananas, strawberries, or mangos, for serving

First, heat up your waffle iron. In a small bowl or in a measuring cup, add the yeast to the warm water and stir to combine. It should start to bubble slightly, and that's how you know it is activating. Set aside while you prepare the rest of the ingredients.

Next, melt the butter in a small pan over medium heat and let cool. In a small bowl, whisk together the flour, sugar, salt, and baking soda to combine. In a larger bowl, whisk together the eggs, almond milk, and the activated yeast. Add the dry ingredients to the wet ingredients and stir to incorporate. Slowly add the melted butter and mix.

In the heated waffle iron, add at least ½ to ¾ cup [120 to 180 ml] of mixture per waffle. Close the iron and let cook for 10 minutes. Remove from the waffle iron and let sit for 3 to 4 minutes before serving.

Serve with maple syrup and fresh fruit. Make these as you need them; they don't store well.

CHAPTER THREE

SANDW AND SALADS

ICHES

Most kids can't stand school lunch. Not me. I loved the sloppy joes, burgers, and peanut butter and jelly sandwiches. It was the one thing that saved me from feeling completely "different." I know, you won't hear many kids say that (not my daughter), but for me, it was true. Thanks to school lunch, my mother didn't pack any aromatic daal or biryani. I could actually blend in a bit more. That was nice. And I ended up in a group of kind of nerdy and kind of cool kids who became my friends. Some of them, like Robby Silk, still are.

Growing up in a traditional Muslim Indian house was not something I would describe as "fun." There was a huge cultural divide between the way I was raised and the way other kids were. Things were just not tolerated in my house. There was discipline. My dad was very strict. We had to pray all the time and go to Sunday school, and it wasn't easy. When kids wanted to sleep over, my mom would say no, or demand two days' notice. I wasn't allowed to go to R-rated movies or have a girlfriend. I wasn't allowed to shave until I was seventeen. Seriously. I had a full-on mustache. It was like that. I always felt like I was missing out.

It was food that brought us all together. My dad would be home late a lot; he worked all the time. But he did love to garden and he

had a green thumb. He grew eggplant, pumpkins, zucchini, tomatoes, chiles, and tons of herbs. And on Saturday or Sunday afternoons, when I wasn't in my room listening to Rush and playing bass, I would help him pick what he grew and bring it inside to my mother in the kitchen.

I liked to help my mom around the kitchen. I didn't do it with any intention that it would be my career; I just liked to be in the kitchen with her. Thinking back on it now, I realize I probably liked it so much because it was very lighthearted. There were no rules. There was no discipline. It was just peaceful. Growing up, we had so many chores—do the dishes, take out the garbage, rake the leaves, cut the grass. We always had so much to do. But when I cooked with my mom, it was one of the few times that I was allowed to just be. To just focus on the cooking. And that was precious to me.

My mom would cook all day, and obviously everything was done by hand. I would do whatever she told me to do. The lessons I learned in her kitchen have stayed with me in every kitchen I've cooked in, whether in my home on the Upper West Side, or side by side with Tom Colicchio at Craft. How to coax the most flavor from your spices (toast them), how to season (take salt in your fingers, don't just shake it or use the palm of your hand), the best way to make rice (soak it for a couple of hours before cooking), and so much more.

On those weekend days, my mom and I would stand together and cook saag paneer; lamb kofta (meatballs); yogurt raita; basmati rice that she made with black cardamom, cloves, and cinnamon; and lentils with cumin, garlic, and ginger. And there was always some roti or flatbread, cooked on the stove top (we had an electric stove, which made it a bit more difficult to get that blistered effect she was used to from an open flame). Those are flavors I never get tired of. It was truly peasant food in every way, but with such elevated, elegant flavors, and it was so satisfying to me. It still is.

These days when I make lunch, whether it's for my daughter or for myself, it's generally at 7 a.m. when I'm not exactly in the mood. As a single dad, I totally get the stress of the morning time crunch, and the added headache of filling that lunch box with meals that are healthy and interesting, but appealing to younger palates. That said, whether you're packing lunch for yourself, or slicing, dicing, slathering, and sandwiching for your kids, there are some easy solutions in this book to add variety and nutrition to your midday meal.

There are lots of ideas in this chapter that will work for school lunch (or in your own lunch box for work). Always pack a variety. I like those bento box–style lunch boxes that give kids a little of everything. I'll add some pasta with Parmesan, peas, and cracked pepper, or leftover Turkey Lasagna (page 138), which is a favorite of Ela's. She loves mozzarella and pesto sandwiches, and sometimes I add a salad with the Ginger Dressing (page 199) with some leftover chicken or turkey. I've also gotten into making pizzas using the Cauliflower Pizza Crust (page 84), Chicken Salad with Radishes, Cherry Tomatoes, Lettuces, and Amazing Caesar Dressing (page 80), and the Yuba Noodle Salad with Ginger Dressing and Raw Vegetables (page 81). Don't be afraid to send breakfast for lunch—Pumpkin Protein Pancakes (page 66) or the Acai Bowl with Fruit and Paleo Granola (page 59). For a treat, I stash some Kabuli Protein Squares (page 178), a container of Paleo Granola with Cashews, Pecans, Almonds, and Figs (page 57), Rice Pudding with Fig Purée and Vanilla (page 174), or Morning Glory Muffins (page 62). Finally, I always add fresh fruit and a note to remind her that I love her.

Braised Lemony Artichoke Salad GF DF VG

If you've never cooked with artichokes, I know it can be intimidating, but once you learn how to turn (clean) one (see facing page), you'll be set, and feel very accomplished. This salad is lemony and bright and tastes like spring.

SERVES 4

FOR THE BRAISED ARTICHOKES

2 tsp extra-virgin olive oil

1 medium carrot, peeled and sliced into thin disks

1 leek, cleaned and sliced (white and pale green parts only)

½ medium Spanish onion, thinly sliced

½ tsp kosher salt, plus more for seasoning

2 artichokes, turned (see facing page)

1 rosemary sprig and 1 thyme sprig in a sachet (see page 95)

1 lemon, cut in half, plus extra juice for holding the turned artichokes

FOR THE SALAD

2 artichokes, turned (see facing page)

10 cups [200 g] mesclun, spring salad mix, or whatever is on hand

1 cup [160 g] cooked red kidney beans

1 cup [240 ml] Lemony Vinaigrette (page 197)

Kosher salt

First, make the braised artichokes. In a medium pot over medium heat, heat the olive oil and add the carrot, leek, onion, and a pinch of salt. Cook for about 5 minutes, until halfway cooked. The vegetables will start to get translucent and soften a bit. Next, add the turned artichokes, the herb sachet, juice of 1 lemon (plus the rest of the lemon), enough water to cover the artichokes, and ½ tsp of salt. Cover with a cartouche (see page 129) or use a lid, slightly askew. Bring to a simmer and cook for 20 to 25 minutes, until the vegetables are tender. Discard the lemon, and cool the artichokes and the vegetables in the braising liquid.

Remove the braised artichokes from the liquid and cut in quarters lengthwise. Remove 1 cup [226 g] of the braised vegetables, drain well, and pat dry.

Now, make the salad. Slice the turned artichokes thinly on a mandoline or by hand. Add the artichokes to a large bowl, along with the lettuces, kidney beans, braised artichokes, braised vegetables, and ½ to 1 cup [120 to 240 ml] of the vinaigrette. Season with a pinch of salt, or more, as desired. Toss well and serve immediately.

GOOD TO KNOW:
How to "Turn" an Artichoke

Turn is the cook's term for cleaning an artichoke. It's a rather lengthy process that no one wants to handle, but when you start out in a restaurant, it's all you do. At home, unless you have a sous-chef (enlist the kids!), here's how it's done: First, pull off all the leaves, including the soft ones in the middle that are on top of the "fuzzy" part of the choke. Cut only about ½ in [12 mm] of the stem off the bottom. Using a paring knife, trim all of the pale green part away from around the choke, keeping the circular shape as you do it. Use a spoon to scrape away the "fuzz," being careful not to scrape into the surface too much. Use your knife to trim the top of any remaining leaves. Carefully trim down the sides and onto the stem. The stem should be shaved down just enough so the dark green color is gone. Immediately put the turned artichokes in cold lemon water until you are ready to cook, otherwise they will oxidize.

Sweet Potato Falafel Salad with Tahini Dressing GF DF V

Chickpeas are a traditional falafel base, but I always find they make falafel too dry. When I revised the recipe with sweet potato and peas, I found the falafel were tastier and had a lot more moisture. This is meant to be a salad but you could also tuck the falafel into pita and add the salad and tahini dressing on top for a fantastic falafel sandwich.

SERVES 4

FOR THE FALAFEL

1 large sweet potato

5 or 6 cilantro sprigs

3½ to 4 cups [70 to 80 g] spinach, packed

1¾ cup [210 g] green peas (defrosted and dried well if frozen)

⅓ cup [43 g or 1.2 oz] coconut flour

1 Tbsp gluten-free flour

1 Tbsp plus ½ tsp vegan butter

1¼ tsp garlic powder

1¼ tsp kosher salt

1 tsp garam masala

1 in [2.5 cm] piece fresh ginger, peeled and minced

1 small jalapeño, seeded and minced

1 tsp canola oil

FOR THE SALAD

10 cups [200 g] mixed lettuces

1½ cups [240 g] cherry or grape tomatoes, cut in half

½ cucumber, peeled and sliced

2 Tbsp torn mint leaves

Kosher salt and freshly ground black pepper

½ cup [113 g] Tahini Dressing (page 202)

Preheat the oven to 375°F [190°C].

First, make the falafel. Wash the sweet potato and poke a few holes in it. Cover with aluminum foil and roast in the oven for 30 to 40 minutes, or until tender. Once it is cool enough to handle, scoop the insides into a medium bowl, and mash by hand or with a mixer. You should have at least ½ cup [113 g] of purée. Let it cool in the refrigerator for an hour to make sure it's cold. You can spread it out on an 8 by 16 in [20 by 40.5 cm] sheet tray to help it cool faster.

Once the purée is cool, add ½ cup of the purée back into the bowl of the food processor, along with all the other falafel ingredients, and process the mixture until completely combined and pretty smooth. It won't be completely smooth, but most large pieces should be broken up at this point.

Next, bake the falafel.

Preheat the oven to 400°F [200°C].

Line an 8 by 16 in [20 by 40.5 cm] sheet tray with parchment paper and spray it with nonstick cooking spray. Measure 2 heaping Tbsp or weigh 1½ oz [40 g] per portion. Roll each portion into a ball and place them on the sheet tray. Bake for 15 minutes, turn the falafel balls over, and bake for another 15 minutes, until caramelized all over. Remove the falafels from the sheet tray and set on a plate at room temperature for 10 to 15 minutes before serving.

While the falafel balls are baking, make the salad. Add the lettuce, tomatoes, cucumber, and mint leaves to a large bowl. Season with 1 tsp of salt (or more as desired) and pepper. Toss with the tahini dressing, using more or less if you'd like. Finish with the warmed falafel.

Store leftover falafel in an airtight container in the refrigerator for up to 1 week, or in the freezer for up to 3 months.

Salmon Salad with Beets and Radishes in a Chia Apple Dressing _{GF DF}

For this salad, I brine the salmon in a mixture of water, chipotle, and salt, which gives the salmon a warm, umami flavor. After the salmon is brined, I coat it with a rub of black pepper and coriander and then bake it. The result will really take you by surprise; it is so incredibly buttery—and yet there's no butter or additional fat. I think (and hope) it will forever change the way you make salmon. I let it cool and flake it over greens with a roasted apple and chia seed dressing, made with shallots and apples caramelized with Dijon and sherry wine vinegar. This is a great salad to serve if friends are coming over for brunch, or for a light weeknight dinner. Open a bottle of white wine and enjoy.

SERVES 4

FOR THE SALMON BRINE

¼ cup [40 g] kosher salt

2 chipotles in adobo

1 tsp dried Mexican oregano, toasted (regular oregano is fine, too)

1 tsp ground allspice, toasted

1 tsp cumin seeds, toasted

1 medium garlic clove

1 lb [455 g] skinless salmon, cut into four 4 oz [115 g] pieces

FOR THE CHIA APPLE DRESSING

¼ cup [60 ml] extra-virgin olive oil

3 medium shallots, thinly sliced

1 apple, peeled and diced

2 Tbsp chia seeds

2 Tbsp sherry wine vinegar

1 Tbsp Dijon mustard

Kosher salt, for seasoning

FOR THE SALMON

2 Tbsp black peppercorns, toasted and ground

2 Tbsp coriander seeds, toasted and ground

Kosher salt

FOR THE SALAD MIX

4 cups [445 g] mixed torn lettuces of your choice (I tend to go with artisan greens or something with the root on it, but mesclun also works!)

5 medium radishes, shaved on a mandoline or sliced into super-thin disks

1 red beet, peeled and shaved on a mandoline or sliced into super-thin disks

½ English cucumber, sliced into coins (I like to partially peel it vertically, leaving some skin on like long stripes)

Kosher salt

First, brine the salmon. In a large glass bowl, combine the salt, chipotles, oregano, allspice, cumin, and garlic with 2 cups [480 ml] of water and whisk to dissolve the salt. Add the salmon fillets and spoon the brine all over. Cover with plastic wrap and refrigerate for 30 minutes.

Preheat the oven to 300°F [150°C].

While the salmon is brining, make the dressing. Heat the oil in a medium saucepan over medium heat, add the shallots, and cook, covered, for 4 to 6 minutes, until the shallots are soft but haven't started to color. Stir in the apple, cover, and cook again until soft, about 6 minutes more. Add the chia seeds, vinegar, and mustard, and stir to combine. Transfer to a blender (or use a handheld immersion blender) and purée for 3 to 4 minutes, scraping down the sides of the blender several times to make sure all the ingredients get fully incorporated. Season with salt. Let cool. (You can pop it in the refrigerator for faster cooling.)

While the dressing is cooling, bake the salmon and assemble the salad ingredients. Remove the salmon from the brine and pat dry. Lay the fillets on a

sheet tray or baking pan and sprinkle both sides with the black pepper and coriander. Season with salt. Bake the salmon for 15 to 20 minutes, or until the internal temperature of the salmon is 145°F [60°C]. Allow the fillets to cool before flaking the salmon.

Next, make the salad. Add the salad greens to a large bowl, toss in the radishes, beet, and cucumber, and season with salt. Add 1 Tbsp of the vinaigrette per serving (so ¼ cup [60 ml] for the entire recipe). This dressing is thick, almost like a Caesar dressing, so it's helpful to use your hands here to really rub the dressing on all the lettuce leaves and other vegetables. Top with the flaked salmon and serve immediately.

Chicken Salad with Radishes, Cherry Tomatoes, Lettuces, and Amazing Caesar Dressing GF DF

Caesar Salad is a classic, but it's not all that good for you. The dressing is very rich and heavy, almost like a sauce. This dressing makes over the classic and keeps all the bright acidity and flavor but lightens things up. It's something I eat all the time for lunch, and even for dinner with some Gluten-Free Bread (page 46) or the Seed Crackers from page 166. For the chicken, I tend to use leftovers from Mexican Roast Chicken with Crispy Skin (page 134), or you can use a store-bought rotisserie chicken, whatever is on hand. Serve this salad on its own or with Tomato Soup with Spanish Lentils and Raisins (page 100) or the Bison Burger with Balsamic Onions and Paleo 1000 Island Dressing (page 86). This salad can be made vegetarian by eliminating the chicken.

SERVES 4

3 to 4 Tbsp [45 to 60 ml] extra-virgin olive oil

1 lb [455 g] oyster, button, or shiitake mushrooms, cleaned and trimmed

1 tsp kosher salt, plus more for seasoning

1 shallot, minced

10 cups [200 g] romaine, frisee, and watercress mix, packed

⅔ cup [80 g] Basic Quinoa (page 42)

½ cup [60 g or 2 oz] chopped and toasted walnuts

1 cup [226 g] roast chicken, pulled from the bone (optional, see headnote)

Freshly ground black pepper

¼ to ½ cup [60 to 120 ml] Amazing Caesar Dressing (page 196)

Start by roasting your mushrooms. In a very hot pan over high heat, add 1 Tbsp of the olive oil and one-third of the mushrooms. Let them sit for a minute undisturbed, then toss them around and let them sit again for about a minute. Add 1 tsp of salt and continue to cook for another 3 minutes or until the mushrooms are tender. You may need to add more oil as you go if the pan gets dry. Add one-third of the shallot during the last 30 to 45 seconds of cooking. Spoon the mushrooms and shallot onto a paper towel to absorb some of the oil. Repeat with the remaining oil, mushrooms, and shallot. You can set them aside in the refrigerator to cool if you prefer your mushrooms cool, or set them on the counter for more room-temperature mushrooms.

Add the romaine, frisee, and watercress mix, the quinoa, walnuts, mushrooms, and chicken (if using) to a medium bowl. Season with salt and pepper and dress with the Caesar dressing.

Yuba Noodle Salad with Ginger Dressing and Raw Vegetables GF DF V

This salad started out as a riff on cold noodles with sesame paste. But when I tried to create a lighter version of the sesame dressing with almond butter, it was too heavy, so I moved toward developing a version of the carrot-ginger dressing I loved from Benihana restaurants. The noodles for this salad are made from yuba noodles created by skimming off the top of warmed soy milk. I like black lentils in this recipe, but you can use another type if you prefer. This salad is light and refreshing and perfect for a hot summer day.

SERVES 4

2 sheets dried yuba noodles

2 tsp dried hijiki

6 cups [120 g] baby arugula

1 small radish, thinly shaved on a mandoline or sliced into super-thin disks

½ small zucchini, thinly sliced into disks

½ cucumber, peeled and thinly sliced into disks

½ carrot, peeled and thinly sliced into disks

½ cup [60 g] Basic Quinoa (page 42)

¼ cup [56 g] black lentils, cooked and cooled to room temperature

Kosher salt and freshly ground black pepper

½ cup [120 ml] Ginger Dressing (page 199)

First, soak the yuba noodles in cold water (enough to cover the sheets completely) for 15 minutes. If they oversoak, they will become very delicate and begin to fall apart. Drain them and place them on paper towels to dry, or carefully pat them dry.

Next, soak the hijiki in enough hot water to cover by 2 to 3 in [5 to 7.5 cm]. Let soak for 6 to 8 minutes and squeeze dry. Roughly chop the hijiki and set aside.

Next, assemble the salad. In a large bowl, add the arugula, radish, zucchini, cucumber, and carrot. Add the quinoa, lentils, yuba noodles, and hijiki.

Season with salt and pepper, and drizzle with the dressing before tossing well. Serve immediately.

Lamb Salad with Guajillo Chile and Paleo 1000 Island Dressing GF DF

Lamb may not be a traditional salad protein, but I love the richness of the meat with the sweetness and crispness of the lettuces and the Paleo 1000 Island Dressing. This recipe requires that you have leftover lamb in the house, so I'd plan on making this salad the day after you've served the Roast Lamb Shoulder with Olive Veracruzana (page 146).

SERVES 4

10 cups [200 g] spinach, radicchio, and butter leaf lettuces, packed

½ apple, thinly sliced

½ red bell pepper, thinly sliced

8 oz [230 g] Roast Lamb Shoulder (page 146)

Kosher salt and freshly ground black pepper

¼ cup [60 ml] Paleo 1000 Island Dressing (page 201)

2 small red beets, peeled and shaved on a mandoline or thinly by hand

Add the lettuces, apple, bell pepper, and Roast Lamb Shoulder to a large bowl. Sprinkle with salt and pepper, add the dressing, then add the beets and mix well. Add more dressing and adjust the seasoning if you'd like. Serve immediately.

Cauliflower Pizza Crust with Seasonal Toppings GF DF V

Cauliflower pizza crusts are everywhere, even Trader Joe's! But I find that most cauliflower crusts have lots of sugar and binders that aren't all that good for you, which inspired me to try to make my own. For this crust, I use coconut flour, which adds a subtle toasted-coconut flavor and is a great binder so the crust stays together quite well. Once you have your crust baked, you have a low-carb base for whatever's in season. In the summer, I like fresh heirloom tomatoes, arugula, Calabrian chile, and Parmesan. In the fall and winter, I go with some roasted mushrooms from the Chicken Salad with Radishes, Cherry Tomatoes, Lettuces, and Amazing Caesar Dressing (see page 80) and grated Pecorino.

SERVES 4

1 cauliflower head (about 2½ lb [1.2 kg])

1 egg

⅔ cup [170 g] Cashew Purée (page 37)

3 Tbsp [24 g or ¾ oz] coconut flour

3 Tbsp [29 g or 1 oz] gluten-free flour

1 tsp dried oregano

¼ tsp kosher salt, plus more for ricing cauliflower

2 tsp extra-virgin olive oil

First, make the cauliflower rice. Trim the green leaves from the cauliflower and cut into large pieces, including the stem. Put a handful at a time in the food processor with enough water to go about halfway up the cauliflower (the water will be drained, but there should be enough so it splashes up the sides when the machine is turned on). Process the cauliflower so it is finely chopped (like rice) and drain the water out. Take out any large pieces and process again in the next batch. Keep doing this until the whole cauliflower is riced. Wrap the cauliflower rice in a kitchen towel or cheesecloth and squeeze well to drain out the extra liquid.

Once the liquid from the cauliflower has been squeezed out as much as possible, combine it with the egg, cashew purée, coconut flour, gluten-free flour, oregano, and salt. The dough should hold its shape when formed in a ball and leave your hands clean.

Preheat the oven to 350°F [180°C].

Line an 8 by 16 in [20 by 40.5 cm] sheet tray with parchment paper and spray it with nonstick cooking spray. Next, form the cauliflower dough into four disks and flatten them on the sheet tray. Press the disks as evenly and thinly as possible without tearing them. Brush with the olive oil and cook for 20 to 30 minutes or until golden brown and fairly dry. Spread your selected toppings on the crust and serve.

Wrap each cooked crust in wax paper and plastic wrap, and store on a flat surface in the refrigerator for 3 to 5 days. They can also be frozen for up to 4 weeks.

Bison Burger with Balsamic Onions and Paleo 1000 Island Dressing GF DF

Bison, if you've never cooked with it, is a super low-fat protein and has a lot of flavor in it. It's a little gamey but not overpowering. It gives you a meaty burger that sears and caramelizes well, without that much fat. I was actually surprised when I had it for the first time. It was so good, but it can be a bit more bloody than red meat, so just be warned. These are wonderful with Roasted Sweet Potatoes with Coconut Oil and Tandoori Masala (page 160).

SERVES 4

FOR THE BALSAMIC ONIONS

2 tsp extra-virgin olive oil

2 large Spanish onions, finely sliced

1 tsp kosher salt, plus more for seasoning

1 rosemary sprig and 2 thyme sprigs in a sachet (see page 95)

1 cup [240 ml] balsamic vinegar

FOR THE BURGER

1 Tbsp canola oil

1 lb [455 g] ground bison

Kosher salt and freshly ground black pepper

4 gluten-free English muffins (or regular if you prefer)

4 Tbsp [56 g] Avocado Aioli (page 191)

4 Tbsp Paleo 1000 Island Dressing (page 201)

4 lettuce leaves

4 tomato slices

First, make the balsamic onions. Add the olive oil to a medium pot over low to medium heat. Add the onions and salt, and cook for 6 to 8 minutes, until the onions become translucent. Add the herb sachet and vinegar. Cover the pot, lower the heat to low, and cook for about 1 hour, stirring occasionally. The vinegar should be completely absorbed and the onions very tender. Season with salt.

Next, make the burgers. Heat the canola oil in a heavy skillet or grill pan over medium heat. While the pan is heating, form the ground bison into four even patties. Season both sides with salt and pepper. Add the burgers and cook for 8 to 10 minutes on each side. They should be medium-well (about 150°F [65°C]) when done. Remove the burgers from the skillet and let them rest for 3 to 5 minutes.

To assemble the burgers, cut the English muffins in half, toast them, and place one burger on the bottom half of each muffin. Top each burger with 1 Tbsp of the avocado aioli, ¼ cup [56 g] of the warm balsamic onions, 1 Tbsp of the dressing, a lettuce leaf, and a tomato slice. Serve immediately. Cooked burgers can be kept wrapped in plastic in the refrigerator for 1 to 2 days.

Black Bean and Sweet Potato Burger with Truffled Mayo GF DF VG

If you're not a fan of veggie burgers, I hope this recipe changes everything. Sweet potatoes are so versatile and good for you (loaded with vitamins A and C), and the black beans add protein, so vegetarians are covered. The combination of the two make this burger tasty and good for you, my favorite combination. I like these burgers with Grilled Corn with Koji Butter (page 157).

MAKES 6 BURGERS

2 medium sweet potatoes

One 15.5 oz [445 g] can black beans, drained, rinsed, and patted dry

1 cup [120 g] Basic Quinoa (page 42)

½ cup [113 g] piquillo peppers, drained well and finely chopped

1 Tbsp plus 2 tsp coconut flour

1½ tsp kosher salt

1 tsp finely minced chipotle in adobo

1 tsp ground cumin, toasted

1 tsp pimenton

1 Tbsp canola oil

6 gluten-free English muffins (or regular if you prefer)

4 Tbsp [56 g] (or more) Truffled Mayo (page 194)

Preheat the oven to 375°F [190°C].

First, make a sweet potato purée. Wash the sweet potatoes and poke a few holes in them. Cover with aluminum foil and roast in the oven for 30 to 40 minutes or until tender. Once they are cool enough to handle, cut the sweet potatoes in half lengthwise, scoop the insides into a medium bowl, and mash by hand or with a mixer. You should have at least 2 cups [453 g] of purée. Let it cool in the refrigerator for an hour to make sure it's cold. You can spread it out on an 8 by 16 in [20 by 40.5 cm] sheet tray to help it cool faster.

While the purée is cooling, add the black beans to a large bowl and mash them with a potato masher or the back of a fork. They don't have to be completely smooth, just broken up, like a thick, chunky paste.

Add the rest of the ingredients through the pimentón to the beans, and combine well. Add the cooled sweet potato purée and continue to mix until cambined. Place the bowl in the refrigerator and chill for at least 15 minutes. Once it's cold, form the mixture into six equal patties.

Next, make the burgers. Preheat the oven to 400°F [200°C].

Heat the oil in a large, heavy-bottomed, ovenproof pan and carefully add the patties (you may have to do half at a time). Let cook on one side for 5 minutes, flip (carefully), and place the pan in the oven for 7 or 8 more minutes. Remove the pan from the oven and let the burgers sit on a cutting board for at least 10 minutes before assembling.

To assemble the burgers, cut the English muffins in half, toast them, and place one burger on the bottom half of each muffin. Top each burger with 1 Tbsp of the mayo and the remaining muffin half and serve.

CHAPTER FOUR

SOUP AND STEW

As I write these pages, I realize I am rapidly closing in on fifty. Getting older is a tough paradox. In many ways, I am at the height of my career, and yet my age sets me apart from the twenty-year-olds in the kitchen. That's part of why this book and these recipes are so important to me: If you take care of yourself and prioritize your health, you can increase your stamina and longevity. For me that means I eat a lot less meat, I try to sleep a little more, I don't eat as much dairy, I drink much less alcohol than I used to, I work out regularly, and I try to continue to do the things that bring me joy. One of those things is playing the bass.

I started out playing drums when I was twelve, but my parents wouldn't buy me a drum set (wonder why). So I gravitated to what was the next best thing—the bass guitar. It gives you the same "bass drum" feeling in your chest. I got very into it very quickly. I was a hyper kid but I wasn't satisfied by playing sports; the bass was my thing and it helped me get that release I craved.

Not long after I started playing, my cousin Farhat was visiting us. He was also very into music and we both had families that didn't quite understand American music and who didn't want us playing it. They thought it was distracting. Farhat brought this cassette tape with him by a band called Rush. It was their *Moving Pictures* album. I listened to it and it changed my life. I'd never heard anything like it. I liked Led Zeppelin and The Kinks but this was my first intro-duction into what a bass could sound like. The notes might have been the same as ones that had been played before, but they sounded different. It was almost like it was a secret you had to be in on to understand the notes. I feel like cooking is very similar. Everyone has the same access to ingredients, but when someone prepares those ingredients just slightly differently and thoughtfully, it can be a revelation.

One night when I was working at Gramercy, where everyone knew I was obsessed with Rush, I was checking the VIP Sheet and saw that Geddy Lee, the bass player from Rush, was set to come in for dinner. I thought that everyone was just messing with me, but they weren't. The band was really coming for dinner. I freaked out. That entire day while waiting for dinner service, I was just losing my mind. When he was finally seated and ordered the tasting menu, I pushed everyone aside and said, "I'm doing his dinner myself." And I made almost every single course on my own. After he finished dinner, he came back to the kitchen and I got to meet him, which was a very special moment, definitely one I will never forget.

While he has nothing to do with my chosen profession, Geddy Lee is my idol. He is still playing and working and performing and has this soulful devotion to bass guitar. He showed me from a very young age how good you can actually get if you apply yourself in that way.

It also makes me think about aging. He is in his late sixties and still on stage going for hours when he is performing live. That's hard on your body, but at the same time, he has never played better. That's the rub about getting older—you get so much better at everything but your body doesn't cooperate the way it used to.

Now, about these soups and stews—these are among my favorite meals to make because they're so versatile. I often make these in advance and heat them up after school when Ela is tired and hungry, but I also rely on them at lunchtime with salad and a nice loaf of bread, or as a starter for a more elaborate supper. These soups may sound like soups you've tried before, but they're all a little surprising because they reflect my mash-up of my culinary leanings— some Mexican, a few Indian, and a couple Mediterranean and Italian. I've also included a basic bone broth, and also a dashi, which I especially love to serve with eggs poached in the broth.

Butternut Squash Soup with Ginger and Chile GF DF V

Butternut squash soup is one of those soups you find on nearly every menu. While I love how silky smooth and almost velvety this soup can get, I find that it tends to straddle the line into dessert. Ultimately, I wanted to bring the emphasis away from the sweetness and into more of the heat of the chiles that I love in Mexican cooking and the warmth of ginger that I use in Indian cooking. I think this will become a fast favorite at your house. I know it is at mine.

SERVES 4 TO 6

1 Tbsp plus 1 tsp extra-virgin olive oil

2 medium garlic cloves, minced

1 large squash, peeled, seeded, and diced

1 medium Spanish onion, minced

2 tsp kosher salt

1 in [2.5 cm] piece fresh ginger, peeled and minced

1 small jalapeño, seeded and minced

1 tsp Arborio rice

1 cup [240 ml] almond milk (plain and unsweetened)

2 Tbsp golden raisins

1 guajillo chile, seeded

1½ tsp tamari

1 tsp fresh lime juice

1 tsp dried Mexican oregano

3 Tbsp almond oil

2 tsp coconut or cider vinegar

Yogurt and toasted pumpkin seeds, for serving (optional)

First, cook the butternut squash. Heat the oil in a large, heavy-bottomed pot over medium heat. Add the garlic, squash, onion, and 1 tsp of the salt. Lower the heat to medium-low and cook for 15 minutes, until the vegetables soften and become translucent.

Next, add the ginger and jalapeño, and cook, uncovered, for another 10 minutes, until everything is soft. Add the rice, almond milk, and 3 cups [720 ml] of water. Bring to a boil and add the raisins, guajillo chile, tamari, lime juice, oregano, and another ½ tsp of the salt. Turn the heat to low and let simmer for 20 minutes.

Next, transfer the soup to a blender, add the almond oil and vinegar, and purée for 3 to 4 minutes, scraping down the sides of the blender several times to make sure all the ingredients get fully incorporated. You could also use an immersion blender, though a regular blender tends to make the soup smoother. Season with the remaining ½ tsp of salt. You may need to add more water if the soup is too thick.

Ladle into soup bowls and garnish with some plain yogurt and toasted pumpkin seeds, if you like, and serve immediately. Store leftovers in an airtight container in the refrigerator for a up to week, or in the freezer for 3 months.

GOOD TO KNOW:
Sachets

Sachets are a subtle way to add more dimension and flavor to soups or other cooking liquids while keeping the herbs neat and tidy; you don't have to worry about fishing stray herbs out at the end. All you need is a piece of cheesecloth and some cooking twine or string. Tuck the herbs inside the cheesecloth, tie it off, and voila, you have your sachet. Kids would probably enjoy making these, so get them involved if you have any running around your house!

Creamy Broccoli and Coconut Soup GF DF V

When I was a kid growing up in Kentucky, my parents used to take me to this restaurant called the Magic Pan. They served mostly crêpes, but my favorite dish on the menu was broccoli Cheddar soup. I had no idea broccoli could taste so good, but then again it was puréed inside a vat of melted cheese.

To achieve that Cheddary richness here, I started out with my Vegan Soubise and added coconut milk, which really imitated that thick and creamy Cheddar soup texture. But that coconut milk led me in a Southeast Asian direction, so I added some curry powder and then pumpkin seeds and almond milk to give it a nuttiness. I like to add brightness right at the end by zesting a lemon on top of the soup. I think your kids might like to eat broccoli after this one.

SERVES 4 TO 6

¼ cup [60 ml] extra-virgin olive oil

11 large garlic cloves, sliced

1 medium Spanish onion, thinly sliced

2 Tbsp Arborio rice

2 to 5 thyme sprigs in a sachet (see page 95)

⅓ cup [45 g] pumpkin seeds

1¼ tsp hemp hearts (see page 24, optional)

1 Tbsp curry powder

One 15 oz [430 ml] can coconut milk

2 cups [480 ml] almond milk

¼ cup [60 ml] Vegan Soubise (page 26)

2 broccoli heads, cut into florets (cut somewhat evenly so that they cook evenly)

1½ Tbsp extra-virgin olive oil

Juice of ¼ lemon

1 Tbsp pumpkin seed oil

2 Tbsp kosher salt, plus more for seasoning

Gluten-Free Bread (page 46), for serving

First, sweat the aromatics. Pour the olive oil into a large stockpot over low to medium heat. Add the garlic, onion, Arborio rice, and thyme sachet, and sweat together for 8 to 10 minutes, until the onion is soft but not colored (the rice will color a bit).

While that's cooking, in a dry pan over medium heat, toast the pumpkin seeds for 2 to 3 minutes, until they start to color and pop. Then add the hemp hearts, if using, and cook for another 1 to 2 minutes. Finally, add the curry powder, cooking for 1 to 2 minutes more. Keep the seed mixture constantly moving in the pan so it doesn't burn.

Add the toasted seed mixture to the sweated onion and garlic. Add the coconut milk, almond milk, soubise, and 3½ cups [840 ml] of water. Simmer over low heat for about 20 minutes, until it's reduced by a quarter.

Next, add the broccoli florets, lower the heat even further so it's just barely a flame, and cover the pot so the florets steam. This will take 7 to 8 minutes, depending on the size of the florets. Be vigilant here; you want the florets to be soft and brightly colored, not mushy and dark green, which will ruin the soup. Let the mixture cool completely. Combine the olive oil and lemon juice. Add the olive oil—lemon juice mixture and pumpkin seed oil. Season with the salt. Transfer the soup to a blender and purée for 3 to 4 minutes, scraping down the sides of the blender several times to make sure all the ingredients are fully incorporated.

Serve with slices of toasted gluten-free bread. Store leftovers in an airtight container in the refrigerator for 3 to 5 days, or freeze for up to 3 months.

Mushroom Dashi GF DF V

Dashi is an incredibly simple broth and one of the foundations of Japanese cooking. It originated more than eight hundred years ago from the combination of Japanese spring water and kombu—a type of kelp—which contains glutamate, the source of dashi's umami flavor. Today it's most classically made with kombu and dried bonito fish, a cousin of tuna, which give the clear broth a sense of the sea. Dashi can be used to make a fantastic bowl of miso soup, or to poach fish or vegetables. This mushroom dashi is meant to be consumed by itself, although I do like to poach an egg in it while it's warming up on the stove, sort of like an egg drop soup. It's also great poured over the Yuba Noodle Salad with Ginger Dressing and Raw Vegetables (page 81) without the dressing, like a healthy ramen. This soup is another one that I make in large quantities; I like to have it on hand throughout the week, especially when the weather is particularly bone chilling.

SERVES 4 TO 6

1 lb [455 g] cremini mushrooms with stems

3 celery stalks, roughly chopped

2 large carrots, peeled and roughly chopped

1 large Spanish onion, peeled and cut into quarters

¼ cup [60 ml] tamari

½ tsp black peppercorns

2 Tbsp dried hijiki

1 tsp kosher salt

Fill a large stockpot with 8 qt [7.5 L] of water. Add the mushrooms, celery, carrots, onion, tamari, and peppercorns. Bring to a boil and add the hijiki. Lower the heat to medium-high and let it simmer for 2 hours. After 2 hours, bring back to a boil for 30 minutes, until the stock is darker and more brown in color. Add the salt and serve.

Store leftovers in an airtight container in the refrigerator for 3 to 5 days, or freeze for up to 3 months.

Moroccan Carrot Soup

This was actually the first soup I developed for Indie Fresh. This carrot soup will surprise you because it's got a lot of body and texture thanks to the Arborio rice and Cashew Purée, which make it thick and creamy without the fat. The quinoa and amaranth add texture and make it feel more like a meal than a soup. This recipe calls for carrot juice, which might have been tough to find a few years ago, but is now readily available at nearly any grocery store. I like this soup on its own, but it also goes well with the Black Bean and Sweet Potato Burger with Truffled Mayo (page 88).

SERVES 4

¼ cup [45 g] amaranth

1 tsp kosher salt, plus more for seasoning

¼ cup [30 g] Basic Quinoa (page 42)

2 tsp coconut oil

6 medium garlic cloves, thinly sliced

2 Tbsp Arborio rice

½ medium Spanish onion, thinly sliced

2 whole cloves, toasted

1 tsp coriander seeds, toasted

½ tsp ground cumin, toasted

Pinch of ground cinnamon

1½ tsp flaxseed

4 cups [960 ml] carrot juice

2 cups [480 ml] almond milk

2 tsp Cashew Purée (page 37)

First, in a small pot, cover the amaranth with cold water (by about 4 in [10 cm]) and add the salt. Simmer for 20 to 30 minutes over low heat, until the amaranth is cooked, and then strain. Measure out ¼ cup [56 g] of the cooked amaranth and set aside with the ¼ cup [30 g] of quinoa.

Meanwhile, in a medium pot over medium heat, melt the coconut oil and sweat the garlic, Arborio rice, and onion for 10 to 12 minutes, until soft. Add the toasted spices, cinnamon, and flaxseed, and continue to cook for another 2 to 3 minutes. Add the carrot juice and let simmer for about 10 minutes. Add the almond milk and let simmer another 10 minutes. Add the cashew purée, stir, and heat long enough to incorporate the purée.

Transfer the soup to a blender (or use an immersion blender) and purée for 3 to 4 minutes, scraping down the sides of the blender several times to make sure all the ingredients get fully incorporated. Pass the mixture through a chinois or fine-mesh strainer back into the pot you cooked it in, and add the cooked quinoa and amaranth. (I use the chinois here to strain out the cloves, and this is more of a broth, so it benefits from the chinois to make it as clean as possible.) Let the soup come back to a boil and season with salt. Serve immediately.

Store leftovers in an airtight container in the refrigerator for 3 to 5 days, or freeze for up to 3 months.

Tomato Soup with Spanish Lentils and Raisins GF DF V

I never liked tomato soup as a kid, maybe because the only version I had was from a can. But when I started working at La Folie in San Francisco after graduating from culinary school, our chef, Roland Passot, made this gorgeous soup from heirloom tomatoes. It was brightened with vinegar and shallots and he used this really rich extra-virgin olive oil. That changed the world of tomato soup for me, and I was inspired to give it another chance. For this soup, I add flaxseed and garlic roasted low and slow in olive oil, which adds depth of flavor as a backdrop to the tomatoes. To give a creaminess without the dairy or the fat, I use tahini. I like soups that have some textures, so I added Spanish lentils. The lentils also turn it into a substantial meal that can work for lunch or dinner with the Chicken Salad with Radishes, Cherry Tomatoes, Lettuces, and Amazing Caesar Dressing (page 80) and a thick slice of Gluten-Free Bread (page 46).

SERVES 4 TO 6

¼ cup [60 ml] extra-virgin olive oil

Cloves from 3 to 4 garlic heads

6 shallots, thinly sliced

2¼ tsp kosher salt, plus more for seasoning

¾ cups [150 g] Spanish lentils

Two and one-half 28 oz [794 g] cans whole tomatoes, drained

½ cup [113 g] Vegan Soubise (page 26)

½ cup [70 g] golden raisins

2½ Tbsp hemp hearts (see page 24)

2½ Tbsp flaxseed

1½ Tbsp tahini

1 Tbsp ground coriander, toasted

¾ Tbsp sherry wine vinegar

First, make a garlicky oil. Add the olive oil and garlic cloves to a medium, heavy-bottomed pot over low to medium heat and roast the garlic cloves until they are golden brown and tender, about 20 minutes. Remove the garlic from the pot and set aside.

In the same pot over medium heat, using all that garlicky oil, add the sliced shallots and ¼ tsp of the salt, and cook until the shallots are caramelized and soft, about 10 minutes.

While the shallots are cooking, in a medium pot, bring 2 cups [480 ml] of water, the lentils, and 1 tsp of the salt to a simmer. Cook the lentils until they are halfway done, 10 to 15 minutes. Strain the lentils and reserve the cooking liquid.

When the shallots are caramelized, add the tomatoes, soubise, raisins, hemp hearts, flaxseed, tahini, coriander, the remaining 1 tsp of salt, and the roasted garlic to the pot. Simmer for 10 minutes. Let it cook down a bit, and then transfer to a blender (or use an immersion blender) and purée for 3 to 4 minutes, scraping down the sides of the blender several times to make sure all the ingredients get fully incorporated.

Wipe out the pot and add the blended soup back into the same pot, along with the lentils and the reserved cooking liquid. Simmer over low heat for 20 to 30 minutes, until the lentils are tender. You may need to add another 1 to 3 cups [240 to 720 ml] of water at this point if it is too thick (it should be a hearty soup consistency).

Season with the sherry wine vinegar and more salt. Serve immediately.

Store leftovers in an airtight container in the refrigerator for 3 to 5 days, or freeze for up to 3 months.

Chicken and Zucchini Soup ^{GF DF}

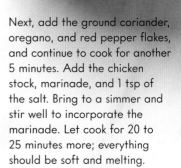

I find zucchini can be kind of bland, which explains why Italians dress up their classic zucchini soup with Parmesan and olive oil. But I like even bigger flavors, so I add Mexican oregano, coriander seeds, and guajillo chiles in the form of My Mexican Marinade (page 41) to give it more complexity. To seed the zucchini, I trim both ends, slice it lengthwise twice to make quarters, then gently run my knife down the length of each quarter to trim the center area with the seeds. It should be diced into about ½ in [12 mm] pieces from there. For the roasted chicken, you can either use leftovers from the Mexican Roast Chicken with Crispy Skin (page 134), or use a store-bought rotisserie chicken. I like to serve this with Gluten-Free Bread (page 46), and if you want a soup and sandwich, serve it with the Black Bean and Sweet Potato Burger with Truffled Mayo (page 88) or the Braised Lemony Artichoke Salad (page 74).

SERVES 6
(MAKES ABOUT 8 CUPS [2 L])

¼ cup [60 ml] extra-virgin olive oil

9 medium garlic cloves, thinly sliced

2 or 3 large zucchini, seeded and diced

1 medium Spanish onion, thinly sliced

2 tsp kosher salt, plus more for seasoning

¾ tsp ground coriander, toasted

¾ tsp dried Mexican oregano, toasted

½ tsp red pepper flakes, toasted and ground

4½ cups [1 L] chicken stock

3½ Tbsp [53 ml] My Mexican Marinade (page 41)

1 cup [226 g] shredded roast chicken

First, heat the olive oil in a medium to large heavy-bottomed pot over medium heat. Add the garlic, zucchini, onion, and 1 tsp of the salt. Sweat 10 for 12 minutes, until the zucchini is tender.

Next, add the ground coriander, oregano, and red pepper flakes, and continue to cook for another 5 minutes. Add the chicken stock, marinade, and 1 tsp of the salt. Bring to a simmer and stir well to incorporate the marinade. Let cook for 20 to 25 minutes more; everything should be soft and melting.

Transfer the contents of the pot to a blender (or use an immersion blender) and purée for 3 to 4 minutes, scraping down the sides of the blender several times to make sure all the ingredients get fully incorporated. Return to the pot, bring to a boil, and add the shredded chicken. Season with salt. Serve immediately.

Store leftovers in an airtight container in the refrigerator for 3 to 5 days, or freeze for up to 3 months.

Roasted Vegetable Soup GF DF V

Vegetable soup is one of those meals, like chicken soup, that just makes you feel better. This one in particular is stocked with lots of veggies and is hearty, nutritious, and filling. I have it around the house when it's a snowy day or just wet and cold outside. Serve this soup with a loaf of Gluten-Free Bread (page 46) or your favorite rustic bread.

SERVES 4 TO 6

8 carrots, peeled and roughly chopped

6 shallots, quartered

2 medium Spanish onions, peeled and cut into quarters

1 fennel bulb, quartered

½ celery bunch, trimmed and roughly chopped

Olive oil

¼ cup [60 ml] tamari

1 star anise, toasted

1 Tbsp ground turmeric, toasted

½ cinnamon stick or a pinch of ground cinnamon, toasted

2 small sweet potatoes, peeled and sliced about ½ in [12 mm] thick

Preheat the oven to 400°F [200°C].

First, toss the carrots, shallots, onions, fennel, and celery in 1 to 2 tsp of olive oil and divide between two 8 by 16 in [20 by 40.5 cm] sheet trays. Roast for 20 to 25 minutes, turning the vegetables over halfway through, until caramelized.

Next, add the roasted vegetables, tamari, star anise, turmeric, cinnamon, and 7½ qt [7 L] of water to a large pot. Bring to a boil and lower the heat to a hard simmer for 1½ to 2 hours. You want to reduce the liquid by half, so it should be simmering hard enough without being at a rolling boil the whole time.

Add the sweet potatoes and simmer for another 30 minutes, until they are just tender. Strain the liquid into another pot to keep warm if you are not going to eat it right away, or straight into serving bowls. Discard the solids.

Store leftovers in an airtight container in the refrigerator for 3 to 5 days or freeze for up to 3 months.

Pho Bone Broth

Bone broth has been around forever, but it hit big a few years back and made its mark because it's pretty powerful protein stock. Bone broth can help alleviate joint and gut pain, boost your immune system, brighten skin, and even make your hair shiny. While it's sold in health food stores, Whole Foods, and famously through a kitchen window now called Brodo at my friend Marco's restaurant Hearth on the Lower East Side of Manhattan, at its essence, it is just really well-made stock. You can make use of any kind of animal bones—beef, chicken, turkey, whatever—which get roasted and then simmered with vegetables for hours (we use marrow in this recipe, but you can feel free to take liberties).

If I feel a cold coming or start to feel run down, I have some for lunch or in the morning before I go out the door. I like it because of the way it makes me feel—satisfied, warmed, and like I'm doing something good for my body and soul. This is something you should make in large quantities, so the recipe is large; you will need a very large stockpot or you can do it in batches. For the fish sauce, I think Red Boat brand is the best to use since it is unsweetened. The bone broth is also great to drink on the go out of a Ball jar.

If you don't have bones on hand for the broth, you can ask your butcher, or get them frozen at Whole Foods.

MAKES 8 CUPS

2½ lb [1.2 kg] beef bones, such as marrow

1 lb [455 g] chicken bones

2½ large Spanish onions, peeled and cut in half

2 celery stalks, cut into large pieces

1 large carrot, peeled and cut into large pieces

½ garlic head, cut lengthwise so the cloves are exposed

1½ Tbsp black peppercorns

15 medium garlic cloves, roughly sliced or slightly crushed

4 whole dates, pitted

2 black cardamom pods or 1 tsp ground cardamom, toasted

1 in [2.5 cm] piece fresh ginger, peeled and sliced into thick coins

1 star anise, toasted

1 cinnamon stick, toasted

¼ cup plus 1 tsp [65 ml] fish sauce

1 tsp kosher salt

¾ tsp dried thyme, toasted

¾ tsp fennel seeds, toasted

½ tsp coriander seeds, toasted

First, make the stock. Add the bones to a large pot of water and bring to a boil. Lower the heat to a simmer and skim off all the impurities (it will look like foam) that come to the top. Skim every 30 minutes, as this is an important step. Let it simmer for another hour.

Add 2 of the onions, the celery, carrot, half a garlic head, and 1 Tbsp of the black peppercorns. Let the stock simmer for another 2 hours, skimming the fat as necessary. Strain the stock.

Roast the remaining half onion directly over the flame of the stove or in the broiler until it is black all over. Add the garlic cloves and the charred onion to a large pot, along with the strained stock and the rest of the ingredients, and bring to a boil. Lower the heat to a simmer and cook for 1½ hours. Strain and discard the solids from the liquid. Serve the broth hot.

Store leftovers in an airtight container in the refrigerator for 3 to 5 days, or freeze for up to 3 months.

Smoked Fish Chowder <small>GF DF</small>

New England clam chowder is delicious, but it's also full of cream, so I never really let myself eat it. To create a version I would feel good eating—one that would be gluten and dairy free—I took out my secret weapon, the Vegan Soubise (page 26). To get that seawater flavor, we use clam juice. I cook the vegetables in this soup just slightly, so they have some tooth and aren't mushy, which no one really wants. For the smoked fish, use smoked trout or another white fish, which you can buy at Whole Foods. Make sure to serve this with oyster crackers, Gluten-Free Bread (page 46), or your favorite bread.

SERVES 4 TO 6

¼ cup [60 ml] extra-virgin olive oil

4 celery stalks, diced

1 medium carrot, peeled and diced

1 medium Spanish onion, diced

9½ cups [2.25 L] clam juice

½ cup plus 1 Tbsp [88 g or 3¼ oz] gluten-free flour

8 oz [230 g] cleaned mushrooms (any type, such as oyster or button), diced

Corn kernels scraped from 2 medium raw cobs

1 cup [240 ml] Vegan Soubise (page 26)

8 oz [230 g] smoked fish, flaked in large pieces

First, sweat the vegetables. Pour the olive oil into a medium to large heavy-bottomed pot over medium heat. Add the celery, carrot, and onion, and cook until the vegetables are halfway cooked, starting to soften, and becoming translucent, 5 to 10 minutes.

While the vegetables are cooking, make a slurry (see facing page) by pouring the clam juice into a large bowl and, while using an immersion blender, slowly adding the flour. Or, use a blender and slowly add the flour to the clam juice as it is blending.

When the vegetables are halfway cooked, pour the slurry on top and let it all simmer for 10 minutes over low heat. Add the mushrooms, corn, and vegan soubise, and cook for another 10 to 15 minutes, until the corn is tender, stirring often. Add the fish and simmer for 10 to 15 minutes more. Remove from the heat and serve right away.

Store leftovers in an airtight container in the refrigerator for 3 to 5 days, or freeze for up to 3 months.

**GOOD TO KNOW:
Slurry**

A slurry is a mixture of some sort of thickener, like flour or corn-starch, and a liquid—anything from water to chicken stock to wine. It's used to give soups a lush texture. Unlike a roux, which is cooked and uses fat to produce a thicker texture, a slurry is made without fat, is uncooked, and is added toward the end of the recipe. We use it in recipes that use gluten-free flour because it's a lot easier to blend gluten-free flour into a sauce when it's incorporated into a slurry.

Gazpacho with Poached Shrimp ^{GF DF}

I find most gazpacho tends to be watery and bland, unless the tomatoes are really stellar. So for this gazpacho, I use a romesco sauce, which gives it a deeper, more complex flavor. The lemon adds a nice jolt of sunshine to the soup, and the poached shrimp make the soup more of a meal, not something that will leave you hungry ten minutes after eating. This is a really light soup, so I might add a salad like the Chicken Salad with Radishes, Cherry Tomatoes, Lettuces, and Amazing Caesar Dressing (page 80) and a loaf of Gluten-Free Bread (page 46).

SERVES 4 TO 6

1 scant Tbsp kosher salt, plus more for poaching

1½ lb [680 g] shrimp (about 25 shrimp), peeled and cleaned

1 Tbsp plus ½ tsp extra-virgin olive oil, plus more for garnishing

1 Tbsp lemon zest

10 or 11 plum tomatoes, cored

1½ cups [340 g] Romesco Sauce (page 33)

1 Tbsp plus 1 tsp sherry vinegar

Freshly ground black pepper (optional)

First, poach the shrimp. Bring a medium pot of water and 1 Tbsp of salt to a boil. Turn the heat down to a very low simmer and add the shrimp. Cook for 3 to 5 minutes, until the shrimp are fully cooked through. Immediately remove the shrimp from the poaching liquid and let cool for 5 minutes. Refrigerate until completely cold, about 30 minutes.

Next, combine the olive oil with the lemon zest. In a blender, combine the tomatoes (leave whole or cut into quarters to fit), romesco sauce, sherry vinegar, olive oil–lemon zest mixture, salt, and water (as necessary if the mixture is too thick). Blend until smooth, about 5 minutes.

When the shrimp are completely chilled, chop into small pieces and mix into the soup. Top with pepper and olive oil, if desired, and serve. The soup can be stored, without the shrimp, in an airtight container in the fridge for up to 3 days.

Chicken and Black Bean Chili GF DF

I'm not a chili person, but I've always loved black beans; they're an excellent plant-based source of protein and they emulate that meatiness you crave. I knew my way into becoming a chili lover was going to be through black beans, which obviously marry well with Mexican flavors. This soup is very filling, so I often serve it for dinner; my daughter, Ela, likes it with Gluten-Free Bread (page 46) and crushed avocado on top.

For the chicken, you can use any combination of legs, thighs, and breast. But it should be about 1 cup [226 g] total of meat, cut into large pieces since it will break down while cooking in the chili and become strings if it's too small to begin with. For 1 cup [226 g] of meat, you'll need about one-quarter of a chicken.

SERVES 4

1 cup [180 g] dried black beans

FOR THE SOFRITO

¼ cup [60 ml] extra-virgin olive oil

7 or 8 medium garlic cloves, peeled

2 plum tomatoes, cored, seeded, and roughly chopped

2 red bell peppers, roughly chopped

1 chipotle in adobo

1 medium Spanish onion, roughly chopped

2 Tbsp dried Mexican oregano

1½ tsp cumin seeds, toasted

1 tsp dried thyme

2 large red bell peppers, cored and seeded

1 cup [240 ml] carrot juice, unsweetened

1 chipotle pepper in adobo, roughly chopped

1¼ cups [300 ml] chicken stock

¼ cup [60 ml] tamari

1½ Tbsp Tomato Paste (see page 31)

1 tsp kosher salt, plus more for seasoning

1 cup [226 g] roast chicken, pulled from the bone (see headnote)

1½ Tbsp Cashew Purée (see page 37)

Gluten-Free Roti (page 45), for serving

½ avocado, sliced, for garnish

Handful of cilantro leaves, minced, for garnish

First, cook and soak the beans. Add the black beans to a large pot and cover with cold water so that the water rises at least 4 in [10 cm] above the beans. Bring to a boil and immediately turn off the heat. Let the pot sit undisturbed for 1 hour, then drain the beans and discard the water.

Meanwhile, make your sofrito. Warm the olive oil in a large, heavy-bottomed pot over low heat. Add the garlic, tomatoes, bell peppers, chipotle, half of the onion, the oregano, cumin, and thyme. Increase the heat to medium and cook for an hour, stirring often, until everything is very soft. Transfer to a blender (or use an immersion blender) and purée for 3 to 4 minutes, scraping down the sides of the blender several times to make sure all the ingredients get fully incorporated.

Next, purée the red bell peppers in a blender to make a pulpy juice. Pour the sofrito in a large pot over medium heat with the red bell pepper juice and carrot juice. Simmer and reduce by half, about 10 minutes.

Next, add the drained black beans, chipotle pepper, chicken stock, tamari, tomato paste, salt, and 3½ cups [840 ml] of water.

Simmer for another 1 to 1½ hours, until the black beans are soft. Add the chicken and simmer another 30 minutes, until the flavors have come together. Stir in the cashew purée and season with salt.

Serve immediately with toasted gluten-free roti, sliced avocado, cilantro, and the remaining chopped onion. Store leftovers in an airtight container in the refrigerator for 3 to 5 days or freeze for up to 3 months.

Feel Better Chicken and Ginger Soup <small>GF DF</small>

One of the best remedies for a cold is ginger; it's an anti-inflammatory that has been used for thousands of years as a natural treatment for colds and flu around Asia. It's also used to help with motion sickness and strengthen immunity. So, if you're sick or feeling like something is coming your way, this is the soup for you. I start out with a traditional chicken soup made from a bone broth that gets turned into edible medicine with the addition of lots of ginger. If you don't have bones on hand for the broth, you can ask your butcher, or get them frozen at Whole Foods. While this soup is delicious on its own, I also like to pour it over Yuba Noodle Salad with Ginger Dressing and Raw Vegetables (page 81) in place of the dressing. Make it for someone you love.

SERVES 4 TO 6

20 lb [9 kg] chicken bones

5 large carrots, peeled and roughly chopped

5 celery stalks, roughly chopped

3 large Spanish onions, peeled and cut in half

1 tsp black peppercorns, toasted

1 bay leaf, toasted

¼ tsp dried thyme, toasted

One 2½ in [6 cm] piece fresh ginger, peeled and cut into ¼ in [6 mm] coins

First, make the stock. Add the bones to a large pot of water and bring to a boil. Lower the heat to a simmer and skim off all the impurities (it will look like foam) that come to the top. Skim every 30 minutes, as this is an important step. Let it simmer for 1 hour, then add 3 of the carrots, 3 stalks of the celery, 2 of the onions, and the peppercorns. Simmer for another 2 hours, skimming the surface every 30 minutes. Strain the liquid and discard the vegetables.

Add 4 qt [3.8 L] of the chicken stock back into the pot, along with the remaining 2 carrots, 2 celery stalks, 1 onion, the bay leaf, and thyme. Simmer for 1 hour and 10 minutes. Add the ginger, and simmer for another 15 to 20 minutes. Strain the liquid and discard the vegetables and aromatics. Serve immediately.

Store leftovers in an airtight container in the refrigerator for 3 to 5 days, or freeze for up to 3 months.

CHAPTER FIVE

WHAT FOR DINNE

'S

R?

Cauliflower with Farro and Coconut Yogurt VG

I'm a big fan of putting vegetables in the center of the plate, and feel like the benefits of a plant-forward lifestyle have led me to serve meatless meals to my family more often. But I'm also someone who likes to feel satisfied, and that's why so many meatless Indian meals work well; they rely on legumes and grains and vegetables that are hearty and super good for you. This Indian cauliflower recipe is one of my favorites. It's like a braised cauliflower and it goes so well with the nutty, chewy farro; and the tang of the coconut yogurt really brightens everything up. If you have a gluten intolerance, don't use the farro, go for Basic Quinoa (page 42) instead.

SERVES 4 TO 6

FOR THE CAULIFLOWER

1 medium cauliflower head, cut into large florets

1 to 2 Tbsp extra-virgin olive oil

2 tsp kosher salt, plus more for seasoning

2 Tbsp coconut oil

2 medium Spanish onions, diced

2 medium garlic cloves, minced

2½ in [6 cm] piece fresh ginger, peeled and minced

1 small jalapeño, seeded and minced

One 14 oz [400 g] can whole tomatoes, gently crushed with your hands

1 tsp ground cumin, toasted

½ tsp ground coriander, toasted

¼ tsp ground turmeric, toasted

¼ tsp red pepper flakes, toasted

FOR THE FARRO

2 Tbsp extra-virgin olive oil

1 medium carrot, peeled and cut in half lengthwise

1 celery stalk, cut in half lengthwise

1 medium Spanish onion, peeled and cut in half

4 cups [907 g] farro

1½ Tbsp kosher salt

FOR THE COCONUT YOGURT

1 cup [240 g] yogurt

½ cup [120 ml] coconut milk

¼ cup [56 g] grated cucumber, liquid squeezed out

¾ tsp ground cumin, toasted and ground

½ tsp kosher salt

Preheat the oven to 450°F [230°C]. Line a sheet tray with parchment paper.

First, toss the cauliflower florets in a large bowl with the olive oil and season with the salt. Spread the florets out on the sheet tray and roast in the oven for 7 to 10 minutes, until the florets start to caramelize and are about halfway cooked. Set aside.

Meanwhile, in a large, heavy-bottomed pot or skillet over medium heat, melt the coconut oil. Spoon in the onions, garlic, ginger, and jalapeño, and slowly cook until they soften, 8 to 10 minutes. Add the tomatoes, cumin, coriander, turmeric, red pepper flakes, and salt (adding 1 tsp of the salt at a time to taste).

Turn the heat to low and cook for 15 to 20 minutes. Add the roasted cauliflower and continue cooking for another 10 to 15 minutes, or until the cauliflower has finished cooking through and is tender when pierced with a fork.

While the cauliflower is cooking, make the farro. Heat the oil in a medium pot over medium heat and add the vegetables. Cook until the vegetables are lightly caramelized, about 5 minutes. Add the farro and cook, stirring frequently, until the farro smells nutty and roasted, 3 to 5 minutes. Add 8 cups [2 L] of water and the salt, and bring to a simmer. Cook, stirring occasionally, until the farro in tender, about 45 minutes. Drain any extra cooking liquid.

Next, make the coconut yogurt. Combine all the ingredients in a medium bowl and mix well. Adjust the seasoning as needed.

To serve, place the cauliflower over the farro and serve the coconut yogurt on the side or over the top. Store leftovers in an airtight container in the refrigerator for 3 to 5 days.

Black Chickpeas and Lentils with Spinach GF DF V

This is my take on a traditional Indian dish called daal chloe. It's a hearty stew that combines chickpeas and lentils with some of my favorite aromatics—cumin, turmeric, ginger, and garlic. It's all braised together for a warm and nourishing weeknight supper. Just be aware that black chickpeas take much longer to cook and don't get super creamy like garbanzos, so you do need to soak them overnight. Serve this with Aromatic Everyday Cauliflower Rice (page 156) and Mango Chutney (page 215).

SERVES 4 TO 6

1 Tbsp coconut oil

2 medium garlic cloves, minced

½ in [12 mm] piece fresh ginger, peeled and minced

2 tomatoes from a can of whole tomatoes, drained well

1 Tbsp cumin seeds, toasted

¾ tsp ground turmeric, toasted

2 Tbsp kosher salt, plus more for seasoning

1 cup [226 g] black chickpeas, soaked in water for 12 hours or overnight

1 cup [200 g] yellow lentils, soaked for 12 hours or overnight

8 cups [160 g] baby spinach

First, heat the coconut oil in a large pot over medium heat and add the garlic and ginger. Cook for 2 to 3 minutes, until the garlic and ginger start to soften. Add the tomatoes, cumin seeds, turmeric, and a pinch of salt, turning the heat to low and breaking the tomatoes gently with a wooden spoon.

Next, add the soaked, drained chickpeas along with 9 cups [2.1 L] of water and the salt. Let this simmer for 30 to 35 minutes or until the chickpeas are three-quarters of the way cooked. They should be soft but have a slight bite to them.

Next, add the soaked and drained lentils. Let this simmer for another 15 minutes or until the lentils and the chickpeas are cooked. The lentils will start breaking down a little bit but shouldn't get completely mushy. Season with salt. Add the baby spinach a handful at a time, letting it wilt and soften. Cook for another 5 minutes. It should be the consistency of a hearty soup. Serve immediately.

Store leftovers in an airtight container in the refrigerator for 3 to 5 days, or freeze for up to 3 months.

Chile Rellenos Stuffed with Amaranth, Quinoa, Almonds, Lemon, and Mint GF DF V

This is one of those traditional Mexican recipes that has been bastardized by chain restaurants so that it's suffocated with heavy sauce and lots of cheese until it's not even recognizable. You can't even tell what's underneath. This is not that. Consider this a spa version of the chile relleno. The grains have a nice texture and the bright lemon zest just makes it really wonderful together. I use poblano peppers for this recipe, which are long and lean and not round and fat like a traditional sweet pepper. But if you have trouble finding them, you can certainly use a red bell pepper instead; just stuff it from the top, not the side. If you can't find jarred squash blossoms, fresh ones are best. If those are not available, use a green or yellow summer squash, and in the winter, you can substitute hearty root vegetables. Serve these with the Guajillo Salsa (page 205) and a squeeze of lemon.

SERVES 4 TO 6

8 poblano peppers

3 Tbsp extra-virgin olive oil

2 medium garlic cloves, thinly sliced

¾ cup [170 g] squash blossoms, left whole

3 cups [360 g] Basic Quinoa (page 42)

1 cup [226 g] cooked amaranth

¾ cup [115 g] coarsely chopped and toasted marcona almonds

Zest of 1 lemon

½ tsp kosher salt

1 Tbsp chopped mint

Lemon wedges, for serving

Preheat the oven to 350°F [180°C].

First, roast the peppers. Place the poblanos directly on the flame of the stove or under the broiler to char the skin. Rotate and move the peppers around so that the whole thing gets deeply charred. Immediately place the peppers in a bowl and cover with plastic wrap. Let sit about 15 minutes.

Meanwhile, in a medium pan, add 1 Tbsp of the olive oil and the garlic. Cook over low heat until soft and lightly browned. Add the squash blossoms and continue to cook for another 5 to 7 minutes. In a large bowl, mix the quinoa, amaranth, almonds, and lemon zest. Add the cooked garlic and squash blossoms, the remaining 2 Tbsp of olive oil, the salt, and mint. Combine well.

Next, lift the plastic wrap off the bowl of peppers and carefully peel the skin off the poblanos, being careful not to make any tears. Slice one side of the poblano, starting at the stem and going down to the bottom, making an opening. Gently pack ¼ to ½ cup [56 to 113 g] of the filling into the poblanos, packing it in all the way to the top, but make sure you're still able to close the pepper.

Line a sheet tray with parchment paper and spray with cooking spray or rub with olive oil. Lay the poblanos, seam-side down, on the tray and bake for 25 to 30 minutes, until hot in the center. Serve with a squeeze of lemon over the top. These don't keep well, so try to eat them immediately.

Cauliflower Rice Biryani GF DF V

Biryani is a traditional baked rice dish from Northern India that typically layers rice and lamb. It's a fairly elaborate meal that requires a day in the kitchen. There's usually a lot of ghee involved, and when my mom made it was usually for a special occasion like Eid, or when company was coming over.

I haven't told my mother about this Cauliflower Rice Biryani recipe, because she tends to get upset when I break from tradition. I remember at Elettaria I made korma, a traditional Muslim dish, with heritage pork. She could not wrap her head around it. She said, "Akhtar, we don't eat pork, so you can't make korma out of pork!" I get it. I suppose it's like making gefilte fish out of shrimp: It just can't be done. But I did it. And it was good.

You can make the cauliflower rice from scratch or just as easily get some from the store. Whatever works for you. You could serve this with Simple Marinated Skirt Steak (page 141), Roast Lamb Shoulder with Olive Veracruzana (page 146), or Mexican Roast Chicken with Crispy Skin (page 134).

SERVES 4 TO 6

1 very large cauliflower head

1 Tbsp plus 1 tsp kosher salt, plus more for seasoning

1 Tbsp coconut oil

2 medium carrots, peeled and diced

1 small red onion, diced

12 whole cloves, toasted

12 cardamom pods, toasted

4 small cinnamon sticks, toasted

½ Tbsp mustard seeds, toasted

½ Tbsp cumin seeds, toasted

2 dried or fresh bay leaves

Mango Chutney (page 215), Coconut Chutney (page 216), and Gluten-Free Roti (page 45), for serving

Preheat the oven to 300°F [150°C].

First, make the cauliflower rice. Trim the green leaves from the cauliflower and cut into large pieces, including the stem. Put a handful at a time in the food processor with enough water to go about halfway up the cauliflower (the water will be drained, but there should be enough so it splashes up the sides when the machine is turned on). Process the cauliflower so it is finely chopped (like rice) and drain the water. Take out any large pieces and process again in the next batch. Keep doing this until the whole cauliflower is riced. Wrap the cauliflower rice in a kitchen towel or cheesecloth and squeeze well to drain the extra liquid.

Pour the cauliflower rice into a large bowl and sprinkle with 1 Tbsp of the salt. Let this sit for 20 minutes to release moisture.

Meanwhile, in a large skillet or pot over medium heat, heat the coconut oil, add the carrots and onion, and sprinkle with the remaining 1 tsp of the salt. Cook for 10 to 15 minutes, until the vegetables are soft. Add the toasted spices and bay leaves and remove from the heat.

By now, the cauliflower should be ready. Wrap it in cheesecloth or a kitchen towel again and squeeze out all the liquid. Make sure you get out as much as possible.

Add the cauliflower rice to the pot of vegetables and spices and stir to combine. Season with salt. Cover with a lid or foil and bake until warmed through, 10 to 12 minutes.

Serve on a large platter or bowl, with the chutneys and gluten-free roti. Store in an airtight container in the refrigerator for up to 3 days.

Verano Ceviche GF DF

You may not think of ceviche as something to make at home, but it's so easy. All it takes is an acid bath of citrus juice and fresh fish diced from your fishmonger. Combine and let it sit for a bit and you have dinner. It's especially nice on a hot summer night when you don't want to turn on the oven. *Aji amarillo* is a yellow chile paste common in Peruvian cooking. They use it almost like a sriracha. You can find it at specialty spice stores like Kalustyan's or Sahadi in New York City. If you can't find it, you can also use a yellow prepared curry paste, or omit it.

SERVES 4

Juice of 10 oranges

Juice of 4 limes

3 Tbsp aji amarillo

1 medium cucumber, sliced into thin rounds

1 small red onion, thinly sliced

1 large radish, cut in half and thinly sliced (should be about 1 cup [226 g])

1 small serrano chile, seeded and minced

Pinch of kosher salt

1 lb [455 g] fish of your choice, cut into ½ in [12 mm] dice

Cilantro leaves and extra-virgin olive oil, for garnish (optional)

Combine all the ingredients through the salt in a large bowl. Pour the mixture over the diced fish and let it sit in the refrigerator for 30 minutes before serving. Garnish with some cilantro leaves and a drizzle of extra-virgin olive oil, if desired. This doesn't keep well, so serve immediately.

Fish Tacos with Pistachio Mole _{GF DF}

For these fish tacos, I prefer a firm, meaty, white-fleshed fish such as mahi mahi, wild striped bass, pompano, or swordfish, which you can bake or broil relatively quickly and serve with this pistachio mole and some tortillas.

SERVES 4 TO 6

FOR THE MOLE

7 tomatillos, husked

2 medium garlic cloves, peeled

½ serrano chile

½ medium Spanish onion

1 whole clove

¼ cinnamon stick

¼ tsp cumin seeds

4 cups [80 g] packed cilantro leaves

⅓ cup [80 ml] extra-virgin olive oil

⅓ cup [45 g] shelled pistachios, toasted

¼ tsp salt

FOR THE FISH

1 lb [455 g] mahi mahi (see headnote), sliced into four 4 oz [115 g] pieces

2 Tbsp The Best Basic Marinade (page 38) or extra-virgin olive oil

Kosher salt

Tortillas, Chipotle Mayonnaise (page 193) and Mango Chutney (page 215), for serving

First, make the mole. On a grill pan or under your broiler, char the tomatillos, garlic cloves, serrano, and onion until deeply charred. Add the clove, cinnamon stick, and cumin seeds, and roast for another minute.

In a medium pot or skillet over low heat, add ½ cup [120 ml] of water and the grilled vegetables and spices, and simmer for 30 minutes. Let cool completely. Pour the contents of the pot into a blender with the cilantro, and blend for 1 minute, until incorporated. Slowly add the olive oil and continue to blend until just combined, about 1 minute. Add the toasted pistachios and salt, and purée until smooth, 1 to 2 minutes more, scraping down the sides of the blender several times to make sure all the ingredients get fully incorporated. Set aside.

Next, make the fish.

Preheat the oven to 350°F [180°C].

Rub the fish all over with the marinade (½ Tbsp per piece of fish) and season with salt. Bake on a sheet tray or in a glass baking dish for 10 to 12 minutes, or until cooked all the way through.

To serve, warm up some tortillas and slather them with mayonnaise. Top the tortillas with the fish and some chutney. Store leftovers in an airtight container in the refrigerator for 1 day.

Halibut with Coconut Sauce GF DF

There actually isn't any coconut used in Northern Indian cooking where my family is from, nor curry leaves, for that matter. These flavors are much more of a Southern Indian thing, but I really love fresh curry leaves and coconut, and so I learned to cook more in that Southern style. This dish features one of my favorite flavor bombs: an intense ginger and tomato confit. When combined with coconut milk and a handful of herbs, such as basil, kaffir lime, and curry leaves, it creates an intense and vibrant sauce that's a great foil for a mild fish like halibut. For the canned tomatoes in this recipe, I like them drained and seeded. You can drain the juice out in a strainer and scrape the seeds out with a spoon or a gloved hand. Serve with a side of Aromatic Everyday Cauliflower Rice (page 156), Braised Romano Beans with Extra-Virgin Olive Oil and Cherry Tomatoes (page 161), or Asparagus with Hazelnuts, Pimenton, and Romesco (page 163).

SERVES 4

3 Tbsp extra-virgin olive oil

3 large garlic cloves, minced

One 1 in [2.5 cm] piece fresh ginger, peeled and minced

1 small or ½ large jalapeño, seeded and minced

1 small Spanish or white onion, minced

1 Tbsp ground turmeric, toasted

1 Tbsp cumin seeds, toasted

One 28 oz [794 g] can whole tomatoes, drained and seeded

One 15 oz [430 g] can coconut milk

4 fresh curry leaves

4 cilantro sprigs

4 mint sprigs

Kosher salt

Four 5 oz [140 g] skinless halibut fillets

¼ tsp Persian lime powder or lime zest

Lime wedges, for serving

Preheat the oven to 350°F [180°C]. Line a sheet tray with parchment paper.

First, make the sauce. Heat 2 Tbsp of the olive oil in a medium saucepan over medium heat. Add the garlic, ginger, and jalapeño, and sauté until tender but not colored (about 2 minutes). Add the onion and sweat for 4 to 5 minutes. Stir in the turmeric and cumin, and cook over medium heat while stirring constantly, about a minute more.

Next, stir in the tomatoes, coconut milk, 1 cup [240 ml] of water, the curry leaves, cilantro, and mint. Simmer over low heat for 20 to 25 minutes, until it has reduced by one-third and has a saucy consistency. Leave to cool slightly before transferring to a blender (or use an immersion blender), and purée for 3 to 4 minutes, scraping down the sides of the blender several times to make sure all the ingredients get fully incorporated. Season with salt (about 1 tsp). Keep the sauce warm in the blender or, if it's still in the pan, reheat it before serving.

Next, prepare the fish. Brush the halibut on both sides with the remaining 1 Tbsp of olive oil and season on both sides with salt and lime powder. Place the fillets on the sheet tray and bake for 10 to 12 minutes or until just cooked through.

Pour the sauce on plates (about ⅓ cup [80 ml] per plate) and serve the fish on top. I like to finish with a squeeze of fresh lime juice just to add a little burst of brightness. If you have leftovers, try to finish them off the next day. Fish is not something I like to keep around for all that long.

GOOD TO KNOW:
What's a Cartouche?

A cartouche is a sheet of parchment paper that you cut to fit over the top of a pot or casserole. It's used as you would use a lid, but the advantage of the cartouche (other than it's fun to say *cartouche*) is that the liquid won't boil away as quickly. This retains moisture in whatever it is you're cooking, and also ensures even cooking. It rests right on top of the ingredients you are cooking. If you don't have parchment or can't be bothered, that's fine. Use a lid just slightly askew.

Cod Piperade ^{GF DF}

The first version of a piperade I cooked was when I was in culinary school in California and worked at Bizou in San Francisco with Chef Loretta Keller, who was my first mentor. Bizou was a Southern Mediterranean place with a beautiful wood-fired oven, and Chef Loretta made piperade in a rustic style with crushed potatoes. It's a simple, relatively clean way to cook fish with lots of flavor from the garlic and pimenton. You can use a cartouche (see page 129) or an actual lid. This recipe calls for pimenton, but it will work just as well with smoked paprika. I suggest serving this with Asparagus with Hazelnuts, Pimenton, and Romesco (page 163) or Crispy Brussels Sprouts with Tamarind and Cashews (page 152).

SERVES 6

1 Tbsp extra-virgin olive oil

2 medium garlic cloves, minced

5 red bell peppers, thinly sliced

2 large Spanish onions, thinly sliced

2 tsp kosher salt, plus more for seasoning

1 cup [240 ml] white wine

½ cup [120 ml] vegetable broth or water

1 tsp pimenton or paprika

2 lb [910 g] cod, sliced into 6 equal portions

Freshly ground black pepper

Preheat the oven to 350°F [180°C].

First, make the piperade. Heat the olive oil in large skillet or pot over low to medium heat and add the garlic. Cook for 1 minute. Add the peppers and onions, stir, season with the salt, and cover with a lid or cartouche (see page 129).

Cook for 12 to 14 minutes, until most of the liquid has evaporated. Add the wine and cover again, cooking until nearly dry, about 8 minutes more. Then add the broth, cover, and reduce until almost dry again, leaving it a little moist but not soaked in liquid. Stir in the pimenton and season with salt. This is your piperade.

Next, cook the fish. Spoon the piperade into a glass or ceramic baking dish, placing the portions of cod on top, and season with salt and pepper (or you can cook this in the pot you used for the piperade if it's ovenproof). Cover with the lid or foil and bake for 10 to 12 minutes or until the cod is completely cooked through. Serve immediately.

Store leftovers in an airtight container in the refrigerator for 1 day.

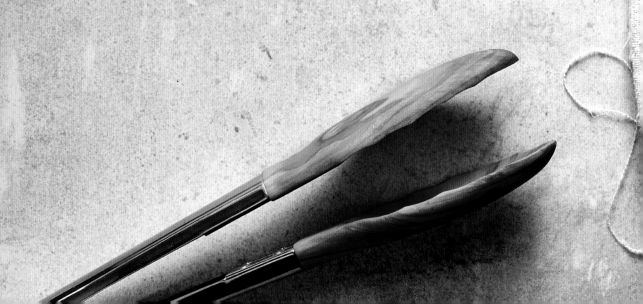

Baked King Salmon with XO Sauce GF DF

When my daughter was really little, it was hard for me to find proteins that she would eat. Eventually she found she liked two—salmon and steak. So I learned to make many different recipes using those two ingredients. This salmon recipe turned out to be her favorite. I like to use wild fish whenever possible because it has so much more flavor than farmed. If you can get king salmon for this, great; if not, Coho is good, too. This sauce is a riff on the classic XO sauce that I discovered on a trip to Hong Kong, traveling with Loretta Keller for an Indian pop-up restaurant. There it is made from dried scallops and shrimp, but I use hijiki and dried shiitakes, which give the sauce a lot of body. It may sound like a strange and exotic sauce, but Ela loves it. This fish is great with Braised Romano Beans with Extra-Virgin Olive Oil and Cherry Tomatoes (page 161) or Roasted Sweet Potatoes with Coconut Oil and Tandori Masala (page 160).

SERVES 4

FOR THE XO SAUCE

1 oz [30 g] dried shiitake mushrooms

1 Tbsp dried hijiki

½ tsp black peppercorns, toasted

½ cinnamon stick, toasted

1 star anise, toasted

1 whole nutmeg, toasted

2 Tbsp extra-virgin olive oil

3 medium garlic cloves, minced

1 shallot, minced

1 in [2.5 cm] piece fresh ginger, peeled and minced

¼ cup [60 ml] tamari

1 chile de árbol

FOR THE SALMON

1½ lb [680 g] wild or king salmon, skin removed, sliced into four 6 oz [170 g] pieces

2 Tbsp black peppercorns, toasted

2 Tbsp ground coriander, toasted

Kosher salt

1 Tbsp extra-virgin olive oil

First, make the sauce. Soak the shiitake and hijiki in separate bowls, covering completely with at least 2 cups [480 ml] of water, for at least 30 minutes or until they are both completely soft. Drain and squeeze both well, reserving 2 cups [480 ml] of the shiitake soaking liquid. Coarsely chop both and set aside.

Meanwhile, grind your toasted spices. Make sure to keep the black peppercorns and coriander for the salmon separate from the spices for the sauce.

In a medium heavy-bottomed pot, heat the olive oil and add the garlic, shallot, and ginger, and sweat over low to medium heat until soft, 5 to 7 minutes. Add the hijiki, shiitakes, tamari, chili de árbol, ground spices, and reserved shiitake soaking liquid. Bring to a simmer and reduce by half, about 20 minutes.

Next, make the fish.

Preheat the oven to 400°F [200°C].

Spoon the sauce into a glass or ceramic baking dish. Season the fish with the ground pepper and coriander and a very small amount of salt (the sauce will be seasoned well already). Place the pieces of salmon on top of the sauce and bake for 8 to 10 minutes, or until the salmon is cooked to your preference. Serve immediately.

Store leftovers in an airtight container in the refrigerator for 3 to 5 days.

Keema Muttar with Peas GF DF

Keema Muttar was the dish that defined my childhood. Think of it as the Indian version of American sloppy joes, or picadillo if you're from Mexico. It was something we ate regularly, and it's still one of my favorite dishes because one bite takes me back to my dining room table in Louisville. Looking back on it now, I feel like one of the reasons my mom made it so often (and that you may as well) is because she was a working parent and this dinner was relatively quick to make. It also stands out from your other "sloppy joe" type meals because it's aromatic with lots of ginger, cumin, and onions. My mom served it with rice and usually string beans or some other vegetable. For this recipe, I've stayed true to the aromatics but used turkey to avoid the richer fatty meat. I was always happy to get this dinner when I was a kid, and even today when I make it for Ela, I feel like I'm home. Serve this with your favorite rice, Aromatic Everyday Cauliflower Rice (page 156), or a stack of warm Gluten-Free Roti (page 45).

SERVES 6 TO 8

2 cardamom pods, toasted

1 small cinnamon stick, toasted

1 tsp ground turmeric, toasted

½ tsp cumin seeds, toasted

½ tsp black peppercorns, toasted

2 Tbsp extra-virgin olive oil or coconut oil

2 lb [910 g] lean, grass-fed, ground dark-meat turkey

1 tsp kosher salt

3 medium garlic cloves, minced

1½ [4 cm] piece fresh ginger, peeled and minced

1 serrano chile, seeded and minced

1 large Spanish onion, thinly sliced

1 dry bay leaf

10 oz [280 g] frozen peas

First, prep the spices. Grind the toasted (and cooled) cardamom pods, cinnamon stick, turmeric, cumin, and peppercorns into a powder in a spice grinder. If you can't fit the cinnamon stick in the spice grinder, break it in half.

Next, in a medium heavy-bottomed skillet over medium heat, warm the oil and then add the turkey. Let it caramelize well, and then stir it up, breaking up the pieces with a wooden spoon as you go. Season with the salt and cook until the liquid has evaporated, 8 to 10 minutes. Drain the turkey, reserving about 2 tsp of the fat in the skillet.

Next, return the turkey to the skillet and add the aromatics—the garlic, ginger, serrano, onion, and ground spices. Turn the heat to low and let it all simmer together until the onion is tender, 5 to 7 minutes, stirring often. Add the bay leaf and peas, increase the heat to medium-low, and cook, uncovered, for 30 minutes, until all the flavors have melded together. Serve immediately.

Store leftovers in an airtight container in the refrigerator for 3 to 5 days, or freeze for up to 3 months.

Mexican Roast Chicken with Crispy Skin GF DF

You're either a believer in brining meat or not. And nonbelievers are, well, just wrong. There's really no other way to make a well-seasoned, juicy chicken that also has a crisp skin. (I also happen to brine my fish. As with meat proteins, brining fish leaves it super buttery and rich, without any fat. Check out the recipe for Salmon Salad with Beets and Radishes in a Chia Apple Dressing (page 78) for more on this.

You'll only need about 3 Tbsp of marinade for this recipe, but you can reserve the rest in a sealed container in the refrigerator for up to 4 weeks. With that leftover marinade, you can make another chicken, or use it on chicken breasts before grilling. I also like to toss it with root vegetables, sweet potatoes, or firm white-fleshed fish like mahi mahi or wild striped bass, marinating them for 10 to 15 minutes before roasting. You could also use this marinade in a stir-fry—just add 1 tsp to bok choy or other stir-fry vegetables and sauté them in the marinade. That's really great, too.

My daughter, Ela, also loves this chicken in a quesadilla with Chihuahua cheese, a great option for any leftovers, pulled from the bone, but it's also great with a number of items, including Crispy Brussels Sprouts with Tamarind and Cashews (page 152), Grilled String Beans with Mojo de Ajo (page 159), or Roasted Sweet Potatoes with Coconut Oil and Tandoori Masala (page 160). Leftover chicken can be used in Chicken Salad with Radishes, Cherry Tomatoes, Lettuces, and Amazing Caesar Dressing (page 80), Chicken and Zucchini Soup (page 102), or Chicken and Black Bean Chili (page 110).

SERVES 4

1 cup [160 g] kosher salt

½ cup [120 ml] agave

1 Tbsp dried oregano, preferably Mexican, toasted

1 chipotle in adobo

One 3 to 4 lb [1.4 to 1.8 kg] whole chicken, tied (see facing page)

3 Tbsp My Mexican Marinade (page 41)

Tortillas, for serving

Guajillo Salsa (page 205), for serving

First, make the brine. In a very large bowl, stir together 4 cups [960 ml] of water, the salt, agave, oregano, and chipotle until the salt and agave dissolve. Transfer the brine and the chicken to a large container or a 2 gal [7.6 L] zip-top bag in which the chicken can be submerged as much as possible in the brine, breast-side down. I tend to prefer a bag just because it's easier to get into the refrigerator. Refrigerate the chicken in the brine for 1 hour.

Toward the end of the brining process, preheat the oven to 400°F [200°C]. Next, remove the chicken from the brine (discard the brine) and pat the chicken dry with paper towels.

Coat the skin of the chicken with the marinade in one even, generous layer, making sure to get some in the cavity of the chicken as well. Put the chicken on a rack set inside a roasting pan. This way the chicken is elevated, air can circulate all around it, and it can brown on all sides.

Roast for 50 to 60 minutes (home ovens vary, so keep an eye on it) or until cooked to an internal temperature of 160°F [71°C]. Keep an especially close eye on the chicken for the last 15 minutes. You want a nice, crispy skin. That said, this particular marinade turns the skin a very dark color, almost like it's been charred, and it's at its most flavorful when it's really dark. Let the chicken rest for about 10 minutes before you slice it.

Serve with warm tortillas and Guajillo Salsa. Store leftovers in an airtight container in the refrigerator for 3 to 5 days.

GOOD TO KNOW:
How to Tie a Chicken

While tying a chicken is not essential, it's a good way to help the bird cook evenly. Now, this doesn't have to be some complicated process; it really can be simple. To tie your chicken, grab some twine and cut two pieces about 3 in [7.5 cm] and 10 in [25 cm] long. Use the short piece to tie the drumsticks together, then trim off the wing tips and tie the long piece of twine around the breast and wings to keep them together. You're done. Now go roast your chicken.

Chicken Tinga GF DF

Chicken tinga is one of Mexico's most beloved street foods. Made with tomatoes, garlic, epazote, onions, and chipotle, it's a comforting stew, sort of their version of ropa vieja or sloppy joes. It's great with cauliflower rice, or you can do it as a filling for tacos with avocado and Guajillo Salsa (page 205). Very often my lunch/breakfast is half an avocado sliced over some tinga with two eggs. My kitchen staff always makes fun of me because I have it all the time, but I never get tired of it.

SERVES 4 TO 6

FOR THE POACHING LIQUID

¼ large Spanish onion (leave the onion quarter whole)

2 medium garlic cloves, crushed

1 bay leaf

1 Tbsp kosher salt

FOR THE TINGA

2 lb [910 g] boneless, skinless chicken thighs

3 Tbsp extra-virgin olive oil

¾ medium Spanish onion, sliced

4 medium garlic cloves, minced

1 bay leaf

1 tsp freshly ground black pepper

2 chipotles in adobo plus 3 Tbsp of the adobo sauce

One 14 oz [400 g] can whole tomatoes, with all of its juices

1 tsp kosher salt

12 tortillas, for serving

½ medium Spanish onion, chopped, for garnish

Handful of cilantro, chopped, for garnish

1 avocado, sliced, for garnish

½ cup Guajillo Salsa (page 205), for garnish

First, make the poaching liquid. In a large pot, add 10 cups [2.4 L] of water, the onion, garlic, bay leaf, and salt, and bring to a gentle simmer over low heat.

While that's going, trim any excess fat off the chicken thighs, if you'd like.

Add the chicken to the poaching liquid and keep it at a very gentle simmer for 15 to 20 minutes, until the chicken is cooked all the way through. Remove the chicken from the liquid and let cool. Reserve 1 cup [240 ml] of the liquid.

In a large skillet, heat the olive oil over medium heat and add the sliced onion and minced garlic. Cook for 10 to 15 minutes, until the onion is soft. Add the bay leaf and black pepper and cook for 1 minute more.

Add the chipotles and adobo, tomatoes, and salt, and cook for 10 minutes, letting the tomatoes break down as they cook. Add ½ cup [120 ml] of the reserved poaching liquid and cook for another couple of minutes. Save the other half of the liquid just in case you need it later on.

By now, the chicken should be cool enough to shred and add to the sauce. Cook the shredded chicken in the sauce for about 15 minutes more, letting the chicken absorb all the

flavors. Adjust the seasoning and add more poaching liquid if needed. It should be moist and fairly saucy but not swimming in a loose sauce.

Serve with warm tortillas, the onion, cilantro, avocado, and Guajillo Salsa. Store leftovers in an airtight container in the refrigerator for 3 to 5 days.

Turkey Lasagna GF DF

We make a fresh gluten-free pasta for this dish, but if the sound of making fresh gluten-free pasta sends you running for the takeout menu, rest assured you can use a store-bought brand of gluten-free pasta (or regular pasta if you don't have any gluten issues).

For the turkey filling, I follow a traditional Bolognese similar to what we did at Craftbar, which is actually Marco Canora's recipe. Marco's Bolognese is still the best I've ever had, but it requires many different meats—pork, veal, and beef. So instead, I use turkey, which is nice and lean, but I follow the same process, with a sofrito of minced carrot, onions, and celery, along with tomatoes. I caramelize the meat and cook it all together. This lasagna is really delicious and something you can make without too much effort on a Sunday afternoon and have it in the house all week.

NOTE: This Bolognese can be made ahead of time and stashed in the refrigerator. It can be frozen, too, and just used as a sauce for pasta, rather than in a lasagna.

SERVES 6 TO 8

FOR THE BOLOGNESE

2 medium Spanish onions, cut into large pieces to fit in the food processor

1 medium carrot, peeled and cut into large pieces to fit in the food processor

1 celery stalk, cut into large pieces to fit in the food processor

4 Tbsp [60 ml] extra-virgin olive oil

4 lb [1.8 kg] ground turkey

Kosher salt

2 rosemary sprigs and 2 thyme sprigs in a sachet (see page 95)

Two 28 oz [794 g] cans diced tomatoes

FOR THE LASAGNA

1 batch Gluten-Free Pasta (page 43) or store-bought lasagna noodles

Kosher salt

1 batch Cashew Purée (page 37)

1 bunch basil leaves

First, make the Bolognese. In a food processor, combine the onions, carrot, and celery, and pulse until they are chopped small, about the size of grains of rice. Spoon the vegetables into a medium Dutch oven or heavy skillet and cover with 3 Tbsp of the olive oil. Heat over medium heat until they start to sizzle, then turn the heat down to low and cover with the lid partly askew, to let in some air. Cook for about

1 hour, stirring occasionally. The vegetables should be a deep bronze color when finished.

Next, heat another medium Dutch oven or heavy skillet with the remaining 1 Tbsp of olive oil over medium heat. Add the turkey and 1 tsp of salt. Cook until the moisture begins to evaporate and the meat begins to caramelize, 6 to 8 minutes. Add the vegetables and cook for 25 to 30 minutes, stirring occasionally.

Add the herb sachet to the meat and vegetables along with the tomatoes. Add 1 tsp of salt and bring to a simmer. Cook for another 35 to 40 minutes. The liquid should be mostly evaporated. Season with salt.

Next, make the lasagna.

Preheat the oven to 350°F [180°C]. Lightly brush a sheet tray with olive oil.

First, cook the pasta. If you're using store-bought pasta, follow the directions on the box to boil the pasta. If you're using the homemade gluten-free pasta, put a large pot of salted water on the stove and bring to a boil.

Meanwhile, roll the pasta into thin sheets on your pasta rolling machine. Layer each sheet with gluten-free flour as you stack them. Cut them into rectangles or squares to fit two per layer in an 11 by 7 in [28 by 17 cm] baking dish. Generously salt the water for blanching and have a large bowl with ice water ready to shock the pasta after being blanched. The pasta should be blanched, one rectangle at a time, for 30 to 45 seconds and then put directly into the ice bath. Layer the rectangles neatly on the sheet tray.

Next, assemble the lasagna. Start with 1½ cups [340 g] of Bolognese spread evenly on the bottom of the baking dish. Next, add the shocked pasta, cutting as needed to fit in one layer. Add another 1½ cups [340 g] of Bolognese.

Thin ⅓ cup [85 g] of the cashew purée with water to the consistency of a béchamel sauce. To make it easy to spread, put it in a piping bag with a medium opening at the tip. You could also use a zip-top bag and cut the corner. Pipe the thinned cashew purée in a zig-zag design to get good coverage on each layer. Next, evenly distribute 2 or 3 basil leaves that have been torn into medium-size pieces. Now repeat the process all over again, starting with the pasta and repeating the layers three more times, ending with the Bolognese on top. Top with a few dollops of the remaining cashew purée (so it resembles pieces of mozzarella cheese) with a torn piece of basil on each dollop.

Bake the lasagna for 30 minutes to 1 hour or until hot all the way through. The timing will really depend on the Bolognese; if it's warm Bolognese, it will take about 30 minutes; if you are using cold ragu, it will take at least an hour to heat all the way through. Store leftovers in an airtight container in the refrigerator for 3 to 5 days.

Bison Meatballs with Cremini Mushroom Sauce and Quinoa GF DF

I created these meatballs when we opened Indie Fresh. Back then, I'd never cooked with bison, but I went with it because it's super lean and high in protein compared to other meats. The problem was, the meatballs were really dry, which was not what I was after. To transform them into something that people wanted to eat, I added eggs and the Cashew Purée (page 37), which made all the difference. I like the slight gaminess of the meat with this mushroom sauce, but you can easily serve these with your favorite tomato sauce or a bright pesto. And if you can't find bison, you can use ground turkey, but try to get it made with both leg and breast meat. These meatballs freeze well and make a relatively quick, easy, and super healthful weeknight dinner for the family.

NOTE: This recipe calls for rice flour, which you can make by buying plain rice crackers (I like the Kame brand Japanese rice crackers) and grinding them in the spice grinder to a flour-like consistency.

SERVES 6

FOR THE MEATBALLS

2 eggs

2 lb [910 g] ground bison

½ cup [113 g] Tomato Paste (page 31) or unsweetened tomato paste

¾ cups [70 g or 2½ oz] rice flour (see Note)

3 Tbsp Cashew Purée (page 37)

1 Tbsp kosher salt

2 tsp curry powder, toasted

FOR THE CREMINI MUSHROOM SAUCE

2 Tbsp extra-virgin olive oil

12 garlic cloves, peeled (about 1 head)

¼ cup [56 g] Tomato Paste (page 31)

3½ Tbsp [53 ml] tamari

¼ cup plus 2 Tbsp [58 g or 2 oz] gluten-free flour

8 oz [230 g] oyster or button mushrooms, cleaned and roughly chopped

Basic Quinoa (page 42)

Preheat the oven to 350°F [180°C].

First, make the meatballs. Lightly beat the eggs in a large bowl. Add the bison, tomato paste, rice flour, cashew purée, salt, and curry powder to the beaten eggs. Gently mix with your hands until all the ingredients are evenly combined. Form into ping-pong-size balls (about 1½ oz [40 g] each) and place onto a wire rack over a sheet tray, so that the fat can drip away while cooking. Space them so that they don't touch each other. Bake for 35 minutes, or until cooked all the way through. The meatballs will look well caramelized and the fat will have dripped away.

While the meatballs are baking, make the sauce. First, add the olive oil and garlic to a medium heavy-bottomed pot over medium heat. Cook until the garlic is golden brown and soft, about 15 minutes. Add the tomato paste, tamari, and 2¾ cups [660 ml] of water, and bring to a boil. Turn the heat to low and use an immersion blender to purée the sauce.

(continued)

While you are blending, slowly add the flour. It clumps up very easily, so make sure to blend while adding small amounts at a time. If you don't have an immersion blender, you can transfer the sauce to a blender and follow the same procedure, but transfer the sauce back to the pot once the flour is incorporated.

Add the mushrooms to the sauce and continue to cook over low heat for about 20 minutes, until the mushrooms are tender, stirring often to avoid burning.

Serve the meatballs on top of the quinoa on a large platter with the sauce poured over the top, or on the side depending on your audience. Store leftovers in an airtight container in the refrigerator for 3 to 5 days, or freeze for up to 3 months.

Roast Lamb Shoulder with Olive Veracruzana ^{GF DF}

Roast lamb with olives is a very traditional Provençal dish, something I'd imagine eating with a hunk of bread and a bottle of wine in the countryside. While I like that image and the traditional French pairing, given my Mexican leanings, I decided to mix things up and do an olive Veracruzana, kind of like a salsa with olives. This would make a standout Easter dinner, or a delicious Sunday supper with friends. Serve this with a side of Aromatic Everyday Cauliflower Rice (page 156) and Braised Romano Beans with Extra-Virgin Olive Oil and Cherry Tomatoes (page 161).

SERVES 4 TO 6

FOR THE BRINE

½ cup [80 g] kosher salt

¼ cup [60 ml] agave

1 Tbsp dried oregano

1 chipotle in adobo

2 lb [910 g] lamb shoulder, cut into 1 in [2.5 cm] pieces

FOR THE LAMB RUB

1 tsp black peppercorns, toasted

¼ tsp ground cumin, toasted

1 tsp ground coriander, toasted

½ tsp fennel seeds, toasted

1 star anise, toasted

FOR THE VERACRUZANA

1 plum tomato

1 serrano chile

1 Tbsp extra-virgin olive oil

15 medium garlic cloves, thinly sliced

2 medium shallots, thinly sliced

½ large Spanish onion, diced

1 cup Castelvetrano olives, thinly sliced

2 Tbsp capers

2 Tbsp chopped cilantro

2 Tbsp guajillo paste

First, brine the lamb. Combine the salt, agave, oregano, and chipotle with 4 cups [960 ml] of water and whisk to dissolve the salt and agave.

Add the lamb and the brine to a large container or zip-top bag. The lamb should be completely covered by the liquid. Refrigerate for 1 hour.

Preheat the oven to 250°F [120°C].

Meanwhile, make the lamb rub. Grind all the cooled, toasted spices together.

Remove the lamb from the brine (discard the brine), pat the lamb dry with paper towels, and toss it with the ground spice mixture. Add the meat to a Dutch oven or a large, ovenproof pot with a lid. The pieces should be in an even layer on the bottom of the pan and not too crowded. Add ½ cup [120 ml] of water, cover, and cook for 2½ to 3 hours, until the lamb is very tender and easily shreds apart.

While the lamb is roasting, make the Veracruzana. Grill the tomato and the serrano on a hot grill or grill pan until charred all over. Place the tomato and serrano in a blender and purée for 3 to 4 minutes, scraping down the sides of the blender several times to make sure all the ingredients get fully incorporated. There's no need to remove the charred parts, they go in the blender, too.

In a medium pan, heat the olive oil over medium heat and add the garlic, shallots, and onion. Cook until soft, 5 to 7 minutes. Add the olives, capers, cilantro, and puréed tomato and serrano. Stir together and add the guajillo paste. Cook for another 10 minutes, until the moisture has cooked out.

Remove the lamb from the oven, let cool on a serving dish, and shred into large pieces.

Spoon the Veracruzana on top; reserve some of the sauce in a bowl so guests can add more if they like.

Store leftovers in an airtight container in the refrigerator for 3 days or freeze for up to 3 months.

CHAPTER SIX

SID

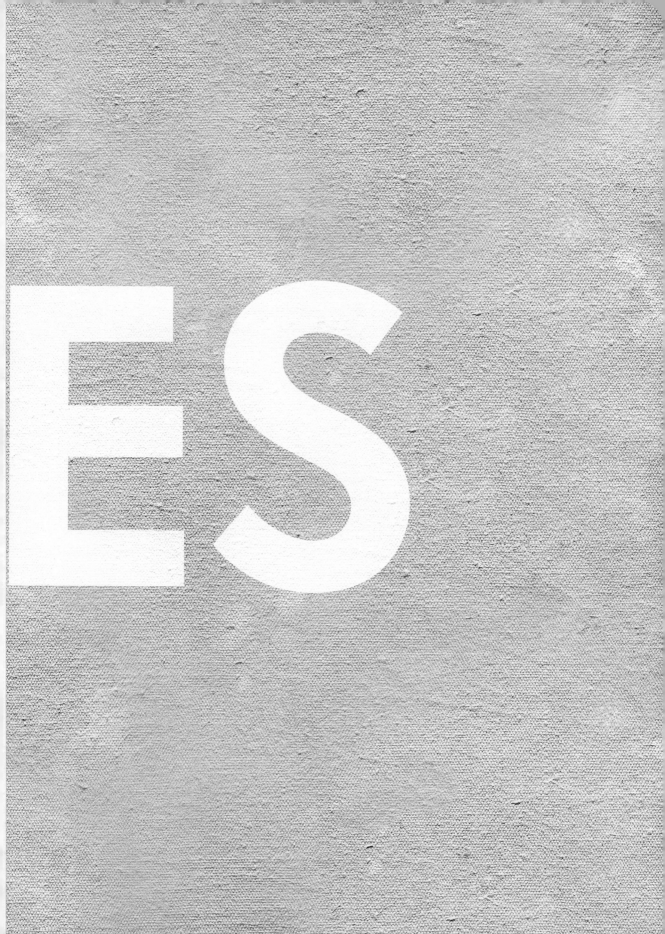

Crispy Brussels Sprouts with Tamarind and Cashews GF DF V

This is one of the Mexican-Indian mashups I created for the menu at my modern Mexican restaurant in Brooklyn, Alta Calidad. I use tamarind, which is traditionally Southeast Asian and Indian but is also used in sodas in Mexico, and added a spicy dry chile pepper called chile de árbol. What I like about these peppers is that they can get really nutty and have a chocolatey aroma. I simmer the tamarind and the chiles down for a while and then purée them into a sauce over the roasted Brussels sprouts. I like to finish the dish with toasted cashews for an additional crunch, but you can leave that out if you have allergies. These would work really well with the Simple Marinated Skirt Steak (page 141) or the Mexican Roast Chicken with Crispy Skin (page 134).

SERVES 4

FOR THE TAMARIND GLAZE

¼ cup plus 1 Tbsp [75 ml] extra-virgin olive oil

4 or 5 large garlic cloves, peeled

1 small plum tomato, sliced lengthwise and seeded

2½ Tbsp unsweetened tamarind paste

2 guajillo chiles

2 small chiles de árbol

1 date, pitted

Kosher salt

FOR THE BRUSSELS SPROUTS

4 cups [453 g] Brussels sprouts, sliced lengthwise and trimmed

2 Tbsp extra-virgin olive oil, plus more for drizzling

1 Tbsp kosher salt

¼ cup [35 g] cashews, toasted and coarsely chopped

Preheat the oven to 475°F [240°C]. Line a sheet tray with parchment paper.

First, make the tamarind glaze. Pour the olive oil into a medium saucepan over low heat and add the garlic. Slowly cook the garlic in the oil until barely golden brown in color, 15 to 20 minutes. The garlic should be soft and easily pierced with a fork. Carefully add the tomato (it might splatter) and cook for another 8 to 10 minutes, until the tomato is very soft and falling apart. Add 1 Tbsp of water, the tamarind, guajillo, chiles de árbol, and date. Increase the heat to medium-high to bring to a boil, turn the heat to low, and simmer for 5 minutes more.

Let cool so it's just warm rather than hot, then transfer to a blender and purée for 3 to 4 minutes, scraping down the sides of the blender several times to make sure all the ingredients get fully incorporated. Season with salt. If the sauce is too thick, you can add another 1 to 2 Tbsp of water. It should be a loose sauce, not quite a vinaigrette, but not super thick either.

Next, make the Brussels sprouts. Toss the Brussels sprouts with the olive oil and salt. Spread them evenly (cut-side down) on the sheet tray and roast in the oven for 12 to 13 minutes or until tender but not mushy.

In a large bowl, toss the roasted Brussels with about 1½ Tbsp of the glaze. Taste and adjust so it suits you. Garnish with the cashews and serve. Store leftovers in an airtight container in the refrigerator 3 days.

Cauliflower with Dukkah and Rice Poha GF DF V

Dukkah is common all over the Middle East, but it is probably best known as an Egyptian spice blend that often contains hazelnuts and sesame seeds along with cumin, coriander, crushed fennel, and black pepper. It's sort of like za'atar in that it gets dusted onto warm breads or sprinkled on yogurt sauces, and it's become so popular that you'll even find it at Trader Joe's.

This recipe is a play on cauliflower with currants, capers, and chile, a classic Italian combination. I started experimenting with this dish at Elettaria and I tweaked it a bit for Alta Calidad to slant it a bit more Mexican. At the restaurant, I add chiles and Mexican oregano and crush everything up so it's almost like a crumble topping for the slow-roasted cauliflower. It's garnished with poha, an Indian snack of cooked sun-dried rice that's been flattened to look like flakes. We use corn for the poha at Alta Calidad, but you could also use corn flakes.

This dukkah mixture is great on fish, sprinkled on salads, and, of course, over plain yogurt. I like it with the Raisin Salsa (page 209). As a side dish, this goes really well with the Simple Marinated Skirt Steak (page 141) and the Halibut with Coconut Sauce (page 128).

SERVES 4 TO 6

FOR THE CAULIFLOWER

2 Tbsp extra-virgin olive oil

1 cauliflower head, Romanesco or regular, cut into small florets

Kosher salt

FOR THE DUKKAH

3 Tbsp [30 g] hazelnuts (about 15 hazelnuts)

1 Tbsp pistachios, shelled (about 18 pistachios)

1 Tbsp sliced almonds, coarsely chopped (you could also use whole almonds, just chop them a little finer so they're consistent with the size of the other nuts)

½ tsp cumin seeds

¼ tsp coriander seeds

¼ tsp fennel seeds

½ tsp sesame seeds

¼ tsp red pepper flakes

2 Tbsp vegetable oil

¼ cup [56 g] corn or rice poha (or unsweetened corn flake cereal)

½ cup [113 g] Raisin Salsa (see page 209)

Preheat the oven to 350°F [180°C]. Line a sheet tray with parchment paper.

First, cook the cauliflower. Heat the olive oil in a large sauté pan over high heat. When the oil is hot, add the cauliflower in a single layer. Work in batches if necessary to avoid overcrowding the pan. Let the cauliflower fry in the oil, undisturbed, for 1 to 2 minutes to get color on the bottom of the florets. Season with salt and toss the cauliflower around in the pan to get more color for about 3 minutes.

Transfer to the sheet tray and continue to cook in the oven for 4 to 5 minutes, until it is just tender enough to pierce with a fork. Remove from the oven and set aside.

Next, make the dukkah. Lower the oven temperature to 300°F [150°C]. Spread the hazelnuts, pistachios, and almonds on separate sheet trays and toast in the oven until lightly browned and fragrant, being careful not to burn them. (The almonds take 4 to 5 minutes, the pistachios 5 to 6 minutes, and the hazelnuts take the longest, 7 to 8 minutes.) Remove the nuts from the oven and let cool. Rub the skin off the hazelnuts after they have cooled. Roughly chop all the nuts and set aside in a big bowl.

Toast the cumin seeds, coriander seeds, and fennel seeds in a dry pan for 3 to 4 minutes, stirring constantly, until fragrant. Transfer to a small bowl and set aside.

Toast the sesame seeds the same way, separately, for 4 to 5 minutes, until lightly browned. Transfer to a separate small bowl to cool.

Finely grind the coriander, cumin, and fennel seeds in a spice grinder. Toss the mixture with the toasted sesame seeds, red pepper flakes, and toasted nuts.

Heat the vegetable oil in a sauté pan over medium-high heat. Once the oil is hot, add the poha, stirring constantly, until browned and crispy, 1 to 2 minutes. Drain on a paper towel. Add the poha to the bowl with the nut mixture and toss together. Leftover dukkah can be stored in an airtight container at room temperature for 1 week.

Top the cauliflower with the salsa and then add some dukkah, about a ¼ cup [56 g] (but use more or less depending on your preference). If you have leftovers, try to keep the elements separate. The cauliflower will keep in an airtight container in the refrigerator for 3 to 5 days, but if it's assembled, it will get mushy and won't keep well.

Aromatic Everyday Cauliflower Rice GF DF V

Cauliflower has become such a trendy vegetable; it's on every menu, whether it's whole roasted, crispy, made into a "steak," or riced. I get why it's taken off—it's gluten-free, low in carbs, naturally high in fiber and B-vitamins, and versatile. The only downside is that it has a lot of water content, so it has the potential to get mushy and can be bland. To make sure this doesn't happen, take the time to get the water out. This way it will be as flavorful as possible with the best texture, too. Serve with anything you would have with rice—Baked King Salmon with XO Sauce (page 132), Black Chickpeas and Lentils with Spinach (page 120), Saag (page 168), or Black Lentils (page 164).

SERVES 4 TO 6

1 large cauliflower head

1 Tbsp kosher salt, plus more for blanching

2 to 3 celery stalks, minced

1 medium Spanish onion, minced

1 large carrot, peeled and minced

First, make the cauliflower rice. Trim the green leaves from the cauliflower and cut into large pieces, including the stem. Put a handful at a time in the food processor with enough water to go about halfway up the cauliflower (the water will be drained, but there should be enough so it splashes up the sides when the machine is turned on). Process the cauliflower so it is finely chopped (like rice) and drain the water. Take out any large pieces and process again in the next batch. Keep doing this until the whole cauliflower is riced. Wrap the cauliflower rice in a kitchen towel or cheesecloth and squeeze well to drain out extra liquid.

Pour the cauliflower rice into a large bowl and sprinkle with 1 Tbsp of the salt. Let this sit for 1 hour to release moisture.

Meanwhile, blanch the vegetables. Line a sheet tray with paper towels. Bring a large pot of water to a boil and generously salt it (use 3 to 4 Tbsp). Add the celery, onion, and carrot and cook for 3 minutes, until just tender. Drain the vegetables in a chinois or fine-mesh sieve and run under cold water to cool. Spread the vegetables on the sheet tray and pat dry.

After the cauliflower has been salted for an hour, put it in a kitchen towel or cheesecloth and squeeze very well until all the liquid is out. Remember, water is your enemy, so take your time here.

Next, combine the cauliflower rice and the vegetables and season with the salt. It's best to combine the vegetables and the cauliflower rice at room temperature for maximum texture and no loss of moisture.

Before serving, warm the mixture in the oven for a few minutes or microwave it just to warm it through. Store leftovers in an airtight container in the refrigerator for 1 day.

Grilled Corn with Koji Butter GF VG

Many Mexican restaurants serve some form of elotes—grilled Mexican street corn slathered with creamy, cheesy, lime-scented, chili-flecked sauce. In this version, I use a cultured koji butter that's so flavorful it's almost like an aged cheese. You could even add chipotle to the koji butter, which would be epic.

SERVES 2

2 corn cobs, shucked
2½ Tbsp Koji Butter (page 28)
Kosher salt

Place the corn cobs directly over the flame of your stove or under the broiler and roast all over, like you would roast a red bell pepper. It should get charred and cooked. Rotate to make sure all sides are evenly charred. This takes about 10 minutes total. You can either melt the butter in a small pan and then brush it on, or rub the unmelted butter on the hot corn. Either way, divide the butter between the corn cobs and season with salt. Serve immediately. This isn't a recipe that really works well for leftovers, so eat it all up.

Grilled String Beans with Mojo de Ajo GF DF V

When string beans get charred they have this amazing smoky flavor. The Mojo de Ajo (page 35) adds so much dimension and body that you may soon find yourself eating these string beans like you do potato chips. Pair them with the Simple Marinated Skirt Steak (page 141) or the Halibut with Coconut Sauce (page 128).

SERVES 4

1 lb [455 g] green beans, trimmed

2 tsp Mojo de Ajo (page 35)

½ tsp kosher salt

1 to 2 tsp canola oil

Lime wedges, for serving

Heat a grill pan or cast-iron skillet over medium to high heat. While the pan is heating, toss your green beans in the mojo de ajo and salt. Add the oil to the pan and add a handful of the beans. You may need to do half or one-third at a time, depending on the pan size—your pan shouldn't be too crowded and the beans should all be touching the surface.

Let them sit for a minute, undisturbed. Toss them once or twice and let them sit again. This time, loosely cover the pan and let them sit for about 3 minutes.

They should have nice char marks and be slightly tender but with a nice bite. Serve with a wedge of lime. This recipe does not keep well as leftovers.

Roasted Sweet Potatoes with Coconut Oil and Tandoori Masala GF DF V

Everyone likes roasted sweet potatoes, and I give them a little Indian kick with tandoori spices and roasted coconut oil, which caramelizes the sweet potatoes really deeply. This would be ideal on a Thanksgiving table, or with the Simple Marinated Skirt Steak (page 141) or the Mexican Roast Chicken with Crispy Skin (page 134).

SERVES 4

3 sweet potatoes, peeled and diced into 1 in [2.5 cm] pieces

2 Tbsp coconut oil

2 Tbsp ground coriander

2 Tbsp sweet paprika

2 Tbsp garam masala

1½ Tbsp kosher salt

1 Tbsp ground cumin

1 Tbsp cayenne pepper

Preheat the oven to 400°F [200°C]. Line a sheet tray with parchment paper.

In a large bowl, toss the diced sweet potatoes with the coconut oil. Add the rest of the ingredients and toss well. Spread the seasoned sweet potatoes on the sheet tray and roast for 50 to 55 minutes, until tender and caramelized. These keep well in an airtight container in the refrigerator for 1 week.

Braised Romano Beans with Extra-Virgin Olive Oil and Cherry Tomatoes GF DF V

Romano beans look like fat string beans; they're also called broad beans or pole beans. They are really meaty and give a bit more texture than skinny string beans. They also hold up well to longer cooking techniques. I first did a version of this dish when I cooked with Marco Canora at Craft, but it was fairly rich, finished with Parmesan and basil. This dish is a little bit lighter. It would go well with the Baked King Salmon with XO Sauce (page 132), the Mexican Roast Chicken with Crispy Skin (page 134), or Simple Marinated Skirt Steak (page 141).

SERVES 4 TO 6

3 Tbsp extra-virgin olive oil

2 to 3 large carrots, peeled and minced

2 celery stalks, minced

1 large Spanish onion, minced

2½ tsp kosher salt

3 pasilla chiles

2 pt [600 g] cherry tomatoes

1 rosemary sprig and 3 or 4 thyme sprigs in a sachet (see page 95)

2 lb [910 g] Romano beans, trimmed

Preheat the oven to 350°F [180°C].

First, heat the olive oil in a large Dutch oven or heavy-bottomed pot over high heat. Add the carrots, celery, onion, and 1 tsp of the salt, and cook over low heat for 15 to 20 minutes, until the sofrito is soft. Stir often.

While the sofrito cooks, toast the pasilla chiles in the oven on a sheet tray for 10 to 15 minutes, until they become brittle. Remove from the oven and, when they're cool enough to handle, crush them with your hands so that they're fine without too many large pieces. Set aside.

Next, add the cherry tomatoes to the sofrito along with another ½ tsp of the salt, and stir. Cook for 5 minutes. Add the pasilla chiles to the pot and stir well.

Add the sachet to the pot along with the beans. Add the remaining 1 tsp of salt, stir well, and cover. Cook for 20 to 25 minutes, stirring often, until the beans are tender.

Transfer the pot with the lid on to the oven and let cook for another hour, until the liquid is absorbed and the beans are very soft. Stir a couple of times during the hour. Adjust the seasoning and serve. Store leftovers in an airtight container in the refrigerator for 3 to 5 days.

Asparagus with Hazelnuts, Pimenton, and Romesco _{GF VG}

This is a great springtime dish. It's my lighter version of the classic asparagus with brown butter and hazelnuts. While this is normally served as a side, I like to put an egg on top and have this for dinner or lunch, but that's just me; I would put an egg on everything. I also like this with the Simple Marinated Skirt Steak (page 141).

SERVES 4

2 tsp extra-virgin olive oil

1 bunch asparagus, trimmed (about 2 in [5 cm] trimmed off the bottom)

½ tsp kosher salt

1 Tbsp Koji Butter (page 28)

2 Tbsp Romesco Sauce (page 33)

1 Tbsp toasted and roughly chopped hazelnuts, for garnish

Pinch of pimenton, for garnish

Lemon wedges, for serving (optional)

Heat a large skillet with the olive oil over medium heat and add the asparagus. Roast for 5 to 8 minutes, until the asparagus is just tender. Add the salt and koji butter to the skillet and toss until melted and coating the asparagus, about 1 minute.

Spread the romesco sauce on the bottom of the plate (either at room temperature or slightly warmed), lay the asparagus on top, and garnish with the chopped hazelnuts and a pinch of pimenton. Serve with a wedge of lemon, if desired. Leftovers do not keep well, so be sure to eat it all up.

Black Lentils ^{GF DF V}

My mom is from Northern India, a region that tends to cook lots of yellow lentils. This style of black lentils is more common in Southern India, so I ate these most of the time when I went to friends' homes who are from that region. While my mom's cooking is the best, I like these lentils because of their earthy flavors. I make this at home a lot. It's great with the Aromatic Everyday Cauliflower Rice (page 156) or regular rice.

SERVES 4 TO 6

8 oz [230 g] whole black lentils

1½ tsp kosher salt

4 canned whole tomatoes and ½ cup [120 ml] of the juice

3 medium garlic cloves, minced

½ in [12 mm] piece fresh ginger, peeled and minced

1½ tsp ground coriander, toasted

1½ tsp garam masala, toasted

1¼ tsp ground cumin, toasted

¼ tsp red pepper flakes, toasted

1 cup [240 ml] almond milk

1½ Tbsp coconut oil

2 Tbsp minced cilantro

First, rinse the lentils (in a chinois or fine-mesh sieve) in cold water until the water runs mostly clear; this takes a few minutes. Add them to a medium to large pot with 3 cups [720 ml] of water and 1 tsp of the salt. Bring to a boil and then turn down the heat to medium so the lentils are simmering gently. Skim off all the foam that rises to the top. Simmer for 35 to 40 minutes, until they are just tender.

While the lentils cook, add the tomatoes, garlic, ginger, and spices to a blender and purée for 3 to 4 minutes, scraping down the sides of the blender several times to make sure all the ingredients get fully incorporated. When the lentils are just tender, add this mixture to the lentils and simmer on low heat for another 20 to 25 minutes (most of the liquid will get absorbed into the lentils).

Next, add the almond milk and simmer for another 15 minutes. Stir in the coconut oil (somewhat vigorously, so it emulsifies), then adjust the seasoning with about ½ tsp of salt and mix in the minced cilantro. Serve immediately. Store leftovers in an airtight container in the refrigerator for up to 3 days.

Lentil Hummus with Seed Crackers

For Prather's on the Alley, my restaurant in Washington, DC, I wanted to serve something for the table that would work well for every diet and restriction. I like hummus but it's everywhere, and I wanted to do something in that vein but a bit less traditional. I went with lentils because they are packed with protein and are so good for you, and also because they reflect a little more of where I come from. I like to use ivory lentils (also called urad) for this hummus, but feel free to substitute any lentils you have on hand.

SERVES 4

FOR THE HUMMUS
1 cup [140 g] ivory lentils
1 Tbsp plus 1 tsp kosher salt
3 Tbsp tahini
3 Tbsp fresh lemon juice
1 small garlic clove
2½ Tbsp extra-virgin olive oil

FOR THE SEED CRACKERS
1¼ cup [283 g] hemp protein
1 cup [160 g] flaxseed
1 cup [140 g] pumpkin seeds
½ cup [56 g] chia seeds
1 Tbsp kosher salt
1 Tbsp coconut oil
2½ Tbsp maple syrup
Sea salt, for sprinkling

First, rinse the lentils (in a chinois or fine-mesh sieve) in cold water until the water runs mostly clear; this takes a few minutes. Add them to a large pot with 4 cups [960 ml] of water and 1 Tbsp of the salt. Bring to a boil over high heat and then turn down the heat to medium so the lentils are simmering gently. Skim off all the foam that rises to the top. Simmer for 20 to 25 minutes, until soft.

Next, transfer the lentils, still in the cooking liquid, to a smaller vessel that can fit in a large bowl filled with ice and water.

This will cool them down quickly. After 15 to 20 minutes, when the lentils have cooled down (they should be at least slightly colder than room temperature by this point), strain the lentils but reserve the cooking liquid.

Add the lentils, tahini, lemon juice, garlic, and 3 Tbsp of the cooking liquid to the bowl of a food processor. Purée for 3 to 4 minutes, scraping down the sides of the food processor to make sure all the ingredients get fully incorporated. Slowly add the olive oil. You may need to add more water if it is too thick. It should be a creamy, hummus-like consistency. Season with salt and serve immediately. Store leftovers in an airtight container in the refrigerator for 1 to 2 days.

Next, make the seed crackers. Preheat the oven to 350°F [180°C]. Line a sheet tray with a silicone baking mat or spray with nonstick cooking spray.

In a large bowl, mix the hemp protein, flaxseed, pumpkin seeds, chia seeds, and salt with ¾ cup [180 ml] of water. Mix until the water is absorbed and the mixture is sticky. With a rubber spatula, spread the mixture on the sheet tray. Use your hands to press down the mixture and make sure it's evenly distributed. It should be about ¼ in [6 mm] thick. Bake for 20 to 25 minutes, until it is set.

It will still seem a little soft at this point, but it will not fall apart when you press it with your finger. Remove the tray from the oven and lower the oven temperature to 325°F [165°C]

Brush the cracker evenly with the coconut oil and maple syrup and sprinkle with some sea salt. Cut the cracker into about 15 large (3 in [7.5 cm]) pieces (you can use the back of the spatula or a dull knife and cut right on the tray) and put the crackers back in the oven and cook for another 20 to 30 minutes, until crispy. The crackers will continue to crisp up as they cool on the sheet tray, but they should be hard when they come out of the oven. Store in an airtight container at room temperature for up to 1 week.

Saag

Saag is a Northern Indian dish with heavy amounts of dairy and cream. I took a lot of time to work on this recipe to bring out as much richness without the traditional ghee and cream. This saag is more like a spinach ragout made with almond milk. This would go well with the Aromatic Everyday Cauliflower Rice (page 156) for a healthy vegetarian dinner. I also like it with the Black Chickpeas and Lentils with Spinach (page 120).

SERVES 4 TO 6

1 Tbsp extra-virgin olive oil

2 medium garlic cloves, thinly sliced

1 medium Spanish onion, thinly sliced

1 in [2.5 cm] piece fresh ginger, peeled and thinly sliced

1 Tbsp Tomato Paste (page 31)

1 Tbsp fenugreek leaves, toasted

1 tsp paprika, toasted

1 tsp ground turmeric, toasted

1 tsp ground cumin, toasted

1 tsp ground coriander, toasted

One 14 oz [400 g] can whole tomatoes, drained and slightly crushed with your hands

1¼ tsp kosher salt

10 oz [280 g] baby spinach

½ cup [120 ml] almond milk

First, heat the olive oil in a medium pot or large skillet over low heat. Add the garlic, onion, and ginger, and cook for 15 minutes, until everything is soft.

Next, add the tomato paste and toasted spices. Stir well and cook for about a minute. Add the tomatoes and 1 tsp of the salt.

Slowly add in the spinach, about a handful at a time, until it is all wilted. Cook for 10 to 15 minutes, until there is no liquid left.

Add the almond milk and turn the heat very low. Let it cook for 20 minutes; most of the almond milk will get absorbed and it will seem almost creamy. Add the remaining ¼ tsp of salt and serve immediately. Store leftovers in an airtight container in the refrigerator for 3 to 5 days.

CHAPTER SEVEN

DESS

ERTS

I have very fond memories of the desserts my mom made for us when I was growing up—the rice pudding and the *gulab jamun*—and I like to make some of them for my daughter. But the Indian desserts of my childhood were creamy and sweet, or sticky and sweet, and they never really called to me. It's not that I shunned dessert—far from it—it was just that I was much more interested in the more traditional American sweets—cookies, cakes, candy bars, ice cream . . . you know what I'm saying, I am sure. When I was growing up I didn't crave Indian dessert. There was nothing I liked more on my birthday than a Mrs. Field's Cookie Cake. I made one for Ela from scratch and it took me back in time. She loved it.

We've talked a lot on these pages about how to maintain health as you age and, for me, that definitely has meant cutting out sweets, nearly universally. It's rare that I sit down with a fudgy brownie, a plate of buttery cookies, a slice of frosted layer cake, or a wedge of fruit pie. Maybe I'll have a lick of my daughter's ice cream cone on a hot day. Not to say these aren't all legit choices; they are, and you should by all means eat desserts like these once in a while. But given that this book is entitled *Good for You*, I haven't included too many classic desserts in this chapter.

What follows are some of my favorite ways to find balance between indulgence and health. So the Rice Pudding with Fig Purée and Vanilla (page 174) is a throwback to the rice pudding my mom made us as kids, but I have used almond milk. The Dark Chocolate Almond Butter Cups with Sea Salt (page 177) are my attempt at a more healthful Reese's Peanut Butter Cup, When I need something sweet at the end of a meal, the Dark Chocolate Truffles (page 179) always call me.

With restaurants in New York City, Alabama, DC, and New Orleans, and projects as far afield as Omaha, I am always on the go. Flying is something I dislike but that I have to do more and more these days. I look at it as an opportunity to get some work done, or to just disconnect and sleep.

Oftentimes my flights aren't that long, but I usually crave something sweet that's kind of a treat, and I tend not to go for the Biscoff Cookies on the flight, even though I actually really love them (don't tell anyone). When I fly, I like to have some natural beef jerky like Dickson's Farmstand; it's high in protein and low in calories. I also always bring some nuts, like almonds and cashews, and my protein powder and a bottle with a ball shaker so I can just add water and be good to go. But I always pack myself a treat, and often it's the Kabuli Protein Squares (page 178). They're crunchy and satisfying and really good for you.

Rice Pudding with Fig Purée and Vanilla GF DF V

Every culture that has rice has some sort of sweet version of rice, and I love rice pudding. My mom made this for us growing up and it was serious fat-boy stuff—with lots of cream and sugar and loaded with almonds, raisins, saffron, cardamom, and cloves. It was so sweet and not very good for you. This version is cleaned up. Instead of relying on sugar, I make a sauce from a store-bought fig purée, vanilla, and dates, which are sweet but are also full of fiber. The Cashew Purée adds that creaminess without the added dairy fat, and the Arborio rice and quinoa add nutrition and a textural note that's more interesting than plain rice.

SERVES 4 TO 6

2¼ cups [540 ml] almond milk

1 cup [200 g] Arborio rice

1 black cardamom pod

½ tsp kosher salt

¾ cup [90 g] Basic Quinoa (page 42)

3 Tbsp chia seeds

2 Tbsp plus 1 tsp maple syrup

1½ Tbsp Cashew Purée (page 37)

FOR THE FIG PURÉE

16 pitted dates

2 cups [453 g] unsweetened fig purée (store bought)

1 Tbsp plus 1 tsp acai juice

1 Tbsp vanilla extract

1 tsp kosher salt

¼ cup [55 g] coconut oil

First, bring 1¼ cups [300 ml] of water, the almond milk, rice, cardamom, and salt to a simmer in a medium pot over medium heat. Stir continuously with a wooden spoon (as if you're making risotto).

After about 15 minutes, the rice should be cooked. Add the quinoa, chia seeds, and maple syrup. Remove the cardamom pod and take the pot off the heat. Stir in the cashew purée to finish. This rice pudding is served cold, so, it should chill in the refrigerator before serving.

While the rice pudding is cooling, make the fig purée. Combine the dates, fig purée, acai, vanilla, and salt in a small pot over medium heat. Bring to a simmer and then whisk in the coconut oil, cooking it all together for 3 to 5 minutes. Transfer to a blender and purée for 3 to 4 minutes, scraping down the sides of the blender several times to make sure all the ingredients get fully incorporated. Refrigerate to cool down.

When you're ready to serve the rice pudding, take it out of the refrigerator and top it with a spoonful of cold fig purée. Store leftovers in an airtight container in the refrigerator for up to 5 days. But come on, it's not going to last that long.

Dark Chocolate Almond Butter Cups with Sea Salt GF DF V

Chocolate and peanut butter is one of my favorite combinations, and I feel like I'm not alone here. When I made desserts for Indie Fresh, I knew I wanted to try to create a version of a Reese's Peanut Butter Cup that I could eat without too much guilt. I think I did a pretty decent job here; this satisfies that primal need for chocolate even though it's seriously good for you.

MAKES 12 INDIVIDUAL CUPS

½ cup [130 g] almond butter (unsweetened, unsalted, and roasted)

1 Tbsp coconut flour

1½ tsp maple syrup

1 tsp sea salt, plus more for garnish

2¼ cups [510 g] vegan dark chocolate chips

¼ cup [60 ml] almond milk

1 Tbsp coconut oil

Line two mini muffin tins with cupcake liners and lightly coat with cooking spray.

Combine the almond butter, coconut flour, maple syrup, and sea salt in a small bowl. Warm in the microwave for about 20 seconds or in a small pot over low heat until it's slightly runny. Put the mixture in a pastry bag or a large zip-top bag (and cut the corner to pipe out the mixture like you would with a pastry bag). Keep this warm in a double boiler over low heat.

Add the chocolate, almond milk, and coconut oil to a large bowl and melt over a double boiler. Stir until completely melted and smooth. Don't let the mixture get too hot, otherwise it will firm up, so keep stirring and don't leave it unattended.

Once it's melted, put the chocolate mixture in another pastry bag or large zip-top bag.

Pipe the chocolate into the cupcake liners, filling them about a quarter of the way. Next, pipe the almond butter mixture into the center of the chocolate. You will want to divide the almond butter evenly between all 12 liners. Next, pipe the chocolate again to cover the almond butter centers. You should see only chocolate on top.

Sprinkle each cup with sea salt and let sit in the refrigerator for at least 1 hour, and serve when chilled. Store leftovers in an airtight container in the refrigerator for up to 2 weeks, but chances are they will get demolished faster than that.

Kabuli Protein Squares ^{GF DF V}

These "cookies" are among my favorite snacks; they add a little bit of sweetness but also boost your energy with protein from the chickpeas. (Don't worry, they don't taste like chickpeas!) I take these on planes with me, pack them in my daughter's lunch box, and have them when I am craving something just a little bit sweet.

MAKES 15 SQUARES

Two 15½ oz [445 g] cans chickpeas, drained, rinsed, and patted dry

¾ cup [170 g] coconut sugar

2 Tbsp plus 1 tsp vegan butter

¼ cup plus 1½ tsp [115 g] maple syrup

2½ tsp vanilla extract

¾ cup [170 g] chia seeds

½ cup plus 1 Tbsp [145 g] almond butter (unsweetened, unsalted, and roasted)

1 cup [156 g or 5½ oz] gluten-free flour

1½ Tbsp almond flour

2 Tbsp vegan protein powder

¾ tsp kosher salt

¼ tsp baking soda

¼ cup plus 2 Tbsp [65 g] vegan chocolate chips

Preheat the oven to 350°F [180°C].

First, in the bowl of a stand mixer fitted with the paddle attachment, mix the chickpeas for 4 to 5 minutes. Start on low speed and as they break up, increase the speed of the mixer to medium-high. You want them to break up and start to get smooth, although they won't get completely smooth.

Next, add the sugar and butter, and beat for another 2 to 3 minutes. Add ⅓ cup [80 ml] of water, the syrup, and vanilla, and continue to mix. Then add the chia seeds and almond butter, followed by both flours (add them slowly so you don't make a huge mess), the protein powder, salt, and baking soda. Mix for another 4 to 5 minutes before adding the chocolate chips, then mix for 1 minute more.

Line an 8 by 11½ in [20 by 29 cm] sheet tray with parchment paper and lightly coat with cooking spray. Spoon the mixture onto the sheet tray and evenly distribute. Use your hands to flatten it and make sure it is even all over. Bake for 25 minutes, until set and hot all the way through. Let cool on the sheet tray before turning out onto a cutting board and cutting into 15 bars. Store leftovers in an airtight container in the refrigerator for up to 1 week.

Dark Chocolate Truffles GF DF V

If chocolate is your weakness, you're welcome. These will satisfy your deepest, darkest need for chocolate and they are so good for you, too. They have a wonderful texture from the hazelnuts, and the cardamom makes them rather elegant.

MAKES 12 TRUFFLES

½ cup [120 ml] coconut milk

1½ tsp vanilla extract

¼ tsp ground cardamom

1½ cups [270 g] vegan dark chocolate chips

Pinch of kosher salt

½ cup [75 g] hazelnuts

Preheat the oven to 350°F [180°C].

In a small pot over medium heat, bring the coconut milk, vanilla, and cardamom to a simmer. Place the chocolate in a medium bowl and immediately pour the hot coconut milk mixture over the chocolate, add the salt, and stir. Keep stirring until the chocolate is completely melted, 5 to 10 minutes. Pour the chocolate into a clean bowl or small dish and let it set in the refrigerator for 30 to 45 minutes.

Meanwhile, place the hazelnuts on a sheet tray and toast in the oven for 7 to 8 minutes, stirring haflway through, or until they are fragrant and slightly more golden in color. When they are cool enough to handle, rub off the hazelnut skins with your fingers and add the hazelnuts to the bowl of a food processor (a mini food processor should work, too). Process until ground but not a fine powder. Spread them out on a large plate.

When the chocolate is firm, use a tablespoon to scoop the truffles. Roll each scoop in your hands to form a ball and then roll the ball in the hazelnuts to coat completely. Work quickly, as the chocolate will melt. Repeat until you have used all the chocolate. Let the truffles set in the refrigerator for about 45 minutes before serving.

Store leftovers in an airtight container in the refrigerator for 1 week.

Protein Kettle Corn GF DF V

This is my favorite snack. I've taken popcorn and turned it into something that is nutritious with chia seeds, flaxseed, hemp hearts, and pumpkin seeds. It has that Cracker Jack sweet-and-salty thing going on. You should bring it to your next ball game.

**MAKES 9 TO 10 CUPS
[200 TO 210 G]**

½ cup plus 1 Tbsp [125 g] coconut oil

1 cup [200 g] organic popcorn kernels

2 Tbsp chia seeds, ground

1 Tbsp plus 1 tsp hemp hearts, ground (see page 24)

1 Tbsp pumpkin seeds, ground

1 Tbsp flaxseed, ground

3 Tbsp maple syrup

Sea salt, for seasoning

Heat the coconut oil in a large pot over high heat to 375°F to 400°F [190°C to 200°C], using a thermometer to keep an eye on the temperature. Add the kernels, cover, and shake the pot around. Once the kernels start popping, keep shaking the pot, and after 3 to 4 minutes of popping, you should be able to slightly lift the lid to stir the popcorn and make sure nothing is burning at the bottom. Keep shaking the pot as much as possible in the meantime. Once the kernels are mostly done popping, pour the popcorn in a large bowl. Set aside.

In a small pan over medium-low heat, toast the ground seeds for about 2 minutes, stirring constantly. Add the maple syrup and stir. Pour the syrup-seed mixture over the popcorn while tossing it (you may want to ask someone to help with this part—one person tosses the popcorn in the bowl while the other pours the syrup). Season with sea salt, and serve. Store leftovers in airtight container at room temperature for up to 1 week.

Matcha Tea Latte ^{GF DF V}

It seems like matcha tea lattes are everywhere lately. That's probably because matcha is such a terrific source of antioxidants; drinking it is sort of like eating an entire green tea leaf (but tastier). Because matcha also produces what's been called a "calm alertness," it's a good alternative to coffee. Many people like this as a dessert, so I have included it here, but I like to have one before I work out in the morning. It gives me a sweet little pick-me-up, which I often need at my age!

SERVES 2

½ cup [120 ml] almond milk

1 tsp matcha tea

3 pitted dates

Ice, for serving

In a small pot over medium heat, bring the almond milk and ½ cup [120 ml] of water to a boil. Whisk in the matcha tea and then add the dates. Let boil for 10 to 15 seconds before removing from the heat. Let the entire mixture cool completely in the refrigerator for about 1 hour or until cold. Transfer to a blender and add another ¼ cup [60 ml] of cold water. Purée for 3 to 4 minutes, scraping down the sides of the blender several times to make sure all the ingredients get fully incorporated. Serve over ice. Leftovers don't keep well, so be sure to drink this right after making it.

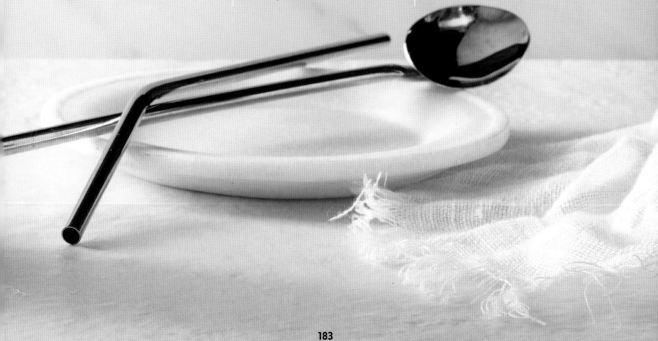

Cardamom Almond Milk GF DF V

I love Mexican horchatas, the icy-cold, milky drink made with rice, flavored with cinnamon, and sweetened with sugar. For this one, I lean on my Indian heritage with a sprinkle of cardamom, and replace the added refined sugar with the natural sugars in dates. It's creamy and rich and makes the perfect frosty summertime drink.

SERVES 2

2 cups [480 ml] almond milk
3 dates, pitted
½ tsp ground cardamom

In a small pot over medium heat, bring the almond milk, dates, and cardamom to a boil. Take off the heat and let sit for 1 to 2 minutes. Transfer to a blender and purée until smooth. Strain the mixture through a chinois or fine-mesh sieve and let cool in the refrigerator. Serve over ice. You could even pop it in a blender and have it frozen like a frappé. Leftovers don't keep well, so be sure to drink this right after making it.

CHAPTER EIGHT

AIOLIS, DRESSIN SALSAS, AND CH

GS,

UTNEYS

MAYOS AND AIOLIS

If you've never made mayonnaise from scratch, it may seem intimidating, but it's so simple and makes such a difference in flavor that you may never reach for the jarred stuff again. Here are a few ways to spice up the basic formula, including an avocado, a curry, a chipotle, and a truffle oil variation. But feel free to use the base as a blank canvas and add whatever is on hand—maybe fresh dill or harissa—and make your own secret sauce.

Avocado Aioli GF DF VG

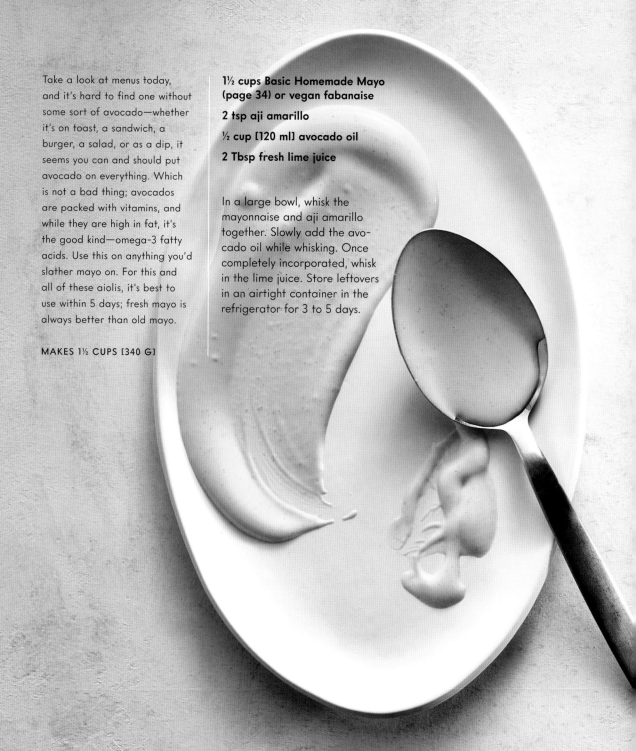

Take a look at menus today, and it's hard to find one without some sort of avocado—whether it's on toast, a sandwich, a burger, a salad, or as a dip, it seems you can and should put avocado on everything. Which is not a bad thing; avocados are packed with vitamins, and while they are high in fat, it's the good kind—omega-3 fatty acids. Use this on anything you'd slather mayo on. For this and all of these aiolis, it's best to use within 5 days; fresh mayo is always better than old mayo.

MAKES 1½ CUPS [340 G]

1½ cups Basic Homemade Mayo (page 34) or vegan fabanaise

2 tsp aji amarillo

½ cup [120 ml] avocado oil

2 Tbsp fresh lime juice

In a large bowl, whisk the mayonnaise and aji amarillo together. Slowly add the avocado oil while whisking. Once completely incorporated, whisk in the lime juice. Store leftovers in an airtight container in the refrigerator for 3 to 5 days.

Curried Aioli GF DF VG

Like many of the aioli recipes in this chapter, this curried version is something you'll reach for over and over again. I think these flavors go particularly well with the Bison Burger with Balsamic Onions and Paleo 100 Island Dressing (page 86), but I also like it on chicken sandwiches to give a more mundane thing a little more personality. It's also a good dipping sauce if you're just making the falafel from the Sweet Potato Falafel Salad with Tahini Dressing (page 76).

MAKES 1½ CUPS [340 G]

1½ cups [340 g] Basic Homemade Mayo (page 34) or vegan fabanaise

1 jalapeño, seeded and thinly sliced

1 medium garlic clove, sliced

1 large shallot, sliced

1 bay leaf

1 Tbsp aji amarillo

½ tsp curry powder, toasted and cooled

Combine all the ingredients in a blender and purée until smooth. Store leftovers in an airtight container in the refrigerator for 3 to 5 days.

Chipotle Mayonnaise GF DF VG

If the only lesson you take from this book is that this Chipotle Mayonnaise should be used on everything and anything, I will feel like I accomplished something important. Seriously though, this mayo is amazing. It's revolutionary on fried chicken, burgers, and nearly any sandwich. You can also use it like a spicy mayo if you make rice balls or sushi at home.

MAKES 1¾ CUPS [396 G]

1½ cups [340 g] Basic Homemade Mayo (page 34) or vegan fabanaise

1 chipotle in adobo

½ small red onion, minced

¼ cup [3 g] cilantro, chopped

1 tsp fresh lime juice

¼ tsp smoked paprika

¼ tsp chile piquin

Add the mayonnaise and chipotle to a blender and purée for 3 to 4 minutes, scraping down the sides of the blender several times to make sure all the ingredients get fully incorporated. Transfer to a medium bowl and add the red onion, cilantro, lime juice, smoked paprika, and chile piquin. Stir until combined. Store leftovers in an airtight container in the refrigerator for 3 to 5 days.

Truffled Mayo GF DF VG

If you're a truffle fan, you'll want to put this on everything you eat. Feel free. This goes really well on the Black Bean and Sweet Potato Burger with Truffled Mayo (page 88).

MAKES ¾ CUP [170 G]

2 Tbsp black truffle oil

¾ cup [170 g] Basic Homemade Mayo (page 34) or vegan fabanaise

¼ tsp fresh lemon juice

Kosher salt

In a large bowl, slowly whisk the truffle oil into the mayonnaise. Whisk in the lemon juice and season with salt. Store leftovers in an airtight container in the refrigerator for 3 to 5 days.

DRESSINGS

These dressings are versatile and add a spark of excitement (and nourishment) to nearly any kind of greens. Many, like the Tahini Dressing (page 202) and the Paleo 1000 Island Dressing (page 201), also work well as a dip for roasted or raw vegetables.

Amazing Caesar Dressing GF DF V

I love a good Caesar salad, but the dressing is also a quick way to turn a salad into a seriously unhealthy meal. I've reformed it in this gluten-free, dairy-free take on the classic. I use walnuts, which emulsify the dressing and add antioxidants, vitamin E, and polyphenols, which are shown to prevent damage from "bad" LDL cholesterol. The dressing gets a jolt of citrus from lemon juice, and even more nutrition from flaxseed, which contain a nice amount of protein, vitamins, fiber, and omega-3 fatty acids. I left the anchovies out to keep it vegan, but if you wanted to add anchovies, feel free.

This dressing is key for the Chicken Salad with Radishes, Cherry Tomatoes, Lettuces, and Amazing Caesar Dressing (page 80), but you can also use it on plain romaine or an ice-berg wedge, or as a dressing for grilled meat and veggies.

MAKES 1 CUP [226 G]

½ cup [60 g] raw, unsalted walnuts

¼ cup [60 ml] fresh lemon juice

2 medium garlic cloves, peeled

1 Tbsp Dijon mustard

1 Tbsp plus 1 tsp red wine vinegar

2 tsp flaxseed

¼ tsp kosher salt

½ cup [120 ml] extra-virgin olive oil

Combine all the ingredients except the olive oil in a blender and purée for 3 to 4 minutes, scraping down the sides of the blender several times to make sure all the ingredients get fully incorporated. Slowly add the olive oil while blending. Continue to blend for another 20 seconds, until the olive oil is fully incorporated.

Store leftovers in an airtight container in the refrigerator for 3 to 5 days.

Lemony Vinaigrette ^{GF DF V}

This is a basic vinaigrette that can be used on any greens you have in the refrigerator—arugula, spinach, kale, what have you. It adds a sunny brightness from the lemon and coriander seeds.

MAKES 1½ CUPS [340 G]

1 Tbsp coriander seeds

½ shallot, minced

¼ cup [60 ml] fresh lemon juice

1 cup [240 ml] extra-virgin olive oil

½ tsp salt

Toast the coriander seeds until aromatic, then lightly crush with a heavy pan or meat tenderizer. Add the crushed seeds to a small bowl, along with the shallot and lemon juice. While whisking, slowly drizzle in the olive oil and salt. Store leftovers in an airtight container in the refrigerator for up to 1 week.

Ginger Dressing

This is a healthier version of the popular carrot ginger dressing served at nearly every Japanese restaurant. This dressing works well with my Yuba Noodle Salad with Ginger Dressing and Raw Vegetables (page 81), but it's also nice on a plain green salad. I like romaine or butter lettuce, the crunchier the lettuce the better, sort of like a Japanese wedge salad.

MAKES 1¾ CUP [396 G]

1 large carrot, peeled and roughly chopped

2 in [5 cm] piece fresh ginger, peeled and minced

½ cup [120 ml red wine vinegar

¼ cup [60 ml] tamari

1 Tbsp plus ½ tsp agave

¼ tsp smoked paprika

½ cup [120 ml] extra-virgin olive oil

First, grind the carrot in a food processor until finely ground. Add the ground carrot to a medium heavy-bottomed pot over medium-high heat along with the ginger, red wine vinegar, tamari, agave, and 1 cup [240 ml] of water.

Bring to a simmer and cook for 20 minutes or until the ginger and carrot are tender.

Let cool slightly, transfer to a blender, and add the paprika. Blend for about 30 seconds and then begin slowly adding the olive oil while the blender is still going. Continue blending until smooth. Store leftovers in an airtight container in the refrigerator for 3 to 5 days.

Paleo 1000 Island Dressing GF DF VG

Thousand Island Dressing originated in New York's Thousand Islands, a collection of picturesque islands between Canada and New York. Legend has it George and Louise Boldt, who summered in the islands, were out for a cruise on their steam yacht, and it was time for lunch. Greens were on the menu, but the Boldts' chef forgot to bring any dressing with him onboard. So, he improvised with what was on hand—whipping together mayonnaise, ketchup, pickle relish, Worcestershire sauce, and a hard-boiled egg.

For this recipe, which I did not create while sailing on a yacht, I use cornichons and their pickling liquid and my homemade Tomato Paste (page 31). It's almost like a tartar sauce. I like this on Lamb Salad with Guajillo Chile and Paleo 1000 Island Dressing (page 83), but it's really great on any sort of salad, with diced-up chicken, shrimp, what have you. It could work with crudité, too.

MAKES 1¾ CUP [396 G]

1 cup [226 g] Basic Homemade Mayo (page 34) or vegan fabanaise

1 plum tomato, cored, seeded, and roughly chopped

2 Tbsp extra-virgin olive oil

1 tsp Tomato Paste (page 31)

10 cornichons, diced

Add the mayonnaise, tomato, olive oil, and tomato paste to the blender. Blend until smooth. Transfer to a bowl and stir in the cornichons. Store leftovers in an airtight container in the refrigerator for 3 to 5 days.

Tahini Dressing

This is another one of those recipes that you will find endless uses for. It's perfect for the Sweet Potato Falafel Salad with Tahini Dressing (page 76) but you can spoon it over grilled chicken, lamb, or steak. Kids love it, too, so put it out with any raw vegetable and watch them eat all their veggies!

MAKES 1 CUP [226 G]

¼ cup [60 ml] fresh lemon juice

¼ cup [56 g] tahini

2 Tbsp extra-virgin olive oil

1½ tsp white sesame seeds, toasted and cooled

½ tsp kosher salt

In a large bowl, whisk the lemon juice and ¼ cup [60 ml] of water into the tahini. Slowly add the olive oil, whisking as you pour it in. Stir in the sesame seeds and salt. Store leftovers in an airtight container in the refrigerator for 3 to 5 days.

SALSAS

If you've traveled to Mexico, you know salsas are at every roadside taco stand and on every table at mealtime. Whether you're making Lean Brisket Tacos (page 140), Mexican Roast Chicken with Crispy Skin (page 134), Roasted Sweet Potatoes with Coconut Oil and Tandoori Masala (page 160), or a simple grilled chicken or fish, adding a salsa or two will make all the difference. Kids also love toppings, so feel free to put them out and encourage them to explore different flavors of the world.

Guajillo Salsa GF DF V

This salsa is fruity and has a little bit of heat, so it's super approachable for any palate. It's obviously terrific with tacos, but you can also use it with Mexican Roast Chicken with Crispy Skin (page 134) or Simple Marinated Skirt Steak (page 141). I also like it as a dip with the Seed Crackers (see page 166).

MAKES 1½ CUPS [340 G]

2 guajillo chiles

1 small chile de árbol

⅛ tsp ground allspice

⅛ tsp black peppercorns

1 garlic clove, peeled

1 plum tomato, cored

½ small Spanish onion, peeled and cut into rings about 1 in [2.5 cm] thick

2 Tbsp golden raisins

⅛ tsp red wine vinegar

½ tsp kosher salt

First, toast the guajillos and chile de árbol in a dry, medium, heavy-bottomed pan over medium-high heat, moving them around frequently, until they darken slightly in color, 3 to 4 minutes. Then add the allspice and black peppercorns and toast for another minute. Remove from the heat and set aside.

Next, turn on the broiler. Set the garlic, tomato, and onion on an 8 by 16 in [20 by 40.5 cm] sheet tray under the broiler and cook until heavily charred all over, turning them over as needed, about 15 minutes. Take the garlic out before the onion and tomato since it will char faster. Add the charred onion, garlic, and tomato to the pan with the guajillos and chile de árbol, along with the raisins and 2½ cups [600 ml] of water. Bring to a boil over high heat and then lower the heat to medium and simmer for 3 to 5 minutes so the mixture is nicely combined and the raisins are plump.

While the mixture is still hot, carefully pour it into a blender, adding the vinegar and salt, and purée for 3 to 4 minutes, scraping down the sides of the blender several times to make sure all the ingredients get fully incorporated. Store leftovers in an airtight container in the refrigerator for 3 to 5 days.

Tomatillo Salsa ^{GF DF V}

Tomatillos, Spanish for "tiny tomatoes," are small and round, vivid green in color, and come wrapped up like little presents in their own papery husks. I love their bright vibrant flavor, which is slightly tart, like the love child of a lemon and a tomato. That sunshine flavor really comes through in this salsa, which I use on all my tacos, but also on my eggs in the morning with some sliced avocado and warmed tortillas. It makes a nice sauce to serve with the Mexican Roast Chicken with Crispy Skin (page 134) or Simple Marinated Skirt Steak (page 141). But it's so versatile and gorgeous in color that it's something I always try to have on the table.

MAKES 1¾ CUPS [396 G]

4 medium garlic cloves, peeled

2 large tomatillos, husked

1 serrano chile, stemmed

**1 small Spanish onion,
cut into 1 in [2.5 cm] rings**

3 cilantro sprigs

1 Tbsp extra-virgin olive oil

1 tsp kosher salt

Fill a medium pot with 2 qt [2 L] of water and add the garlic, tomatillos, serrano, and onion. Bring to a boil over high heat and then lower the heat to medium and simmer for 20 to 25 minutes, until everything is tender. Drain and discard the liquid. Add just the solids, along with the cilantro sprigs, to a blender with the olive oil and salt and purée for 3 to 4 minutes, scraping down the sides of the blender several times to make sure all the ingredients get fully incorporated.

Store leftovers in an airtight container in the refrigerator for 3 to 5 days.

Raisin Salsa ^{GF DF V}

This salsa, which I serve with Cauliflower with Dukkah and Rice Poha (page 154), is a play on a traditional Sicilian pairing of cauliflower and raisins. The raisins soften and get plumped up in this recipe, and their sweetness, combined with the nuttiness of the dukkah, is a terrific marriage of textures and flavors. This salsa is also a simple way to liven up roasted meats and would be great with Lamb Salad with Guajillo Chile and Paleo 1000 Island Dressing (page 83).

MAKES 1 CUP [226 G]

1 Tbsp extra-virgin olive oil, plus more as needed

1 small Spanish onion, minced

½ serrano chile, seeded and minced

Pinch of kosher salt

½ cup [70 g] golden raisins

½ cup [120 ml] fresh orange juice (from 3 small oranges)

1 tsp cider vinegar

First, heat the olive oil in a saucepan over medium heat until glistening. Add the onion and chile and sweat until soft, not letting the onion brown. Season with the salt. Cook for 5 to 6 minutes more, adding more olive oil, if needed, to prevent burning.

Next, add the raisins, orange juice, and vinegar. Bring to a boil, then turn the heat to a low simmer. Let the mixture simmer until almost all the liquid is absorbed, about 12 minutes. Let it cool to room temperature.

Store leftovers in an airtight container in the refrigerator for 3 to 5 days.

CHUTNEYS AND MORE

When you go out for Korean food, the table is always adorned with a collection of little dishes called *bon chan*—pungent condiments and pickles to share. The Indian table is similar; we always serve chutneys, kachumber, and raita as part of the meal. All the toppings give meals a sense of fun and adventure!

Raita GF VG

Raita is a traditional Northern Indian condiment made from grated cucumber and yogurt. For this version, I lighten it up with olive oil. A lot of raita recipes contain sugar, which is something I have omitted. Raita is great to cut the heat of a dish, and is also used because it has a probiotic quality and can help with digestion. I love this with the Roast Lamb Shoulder with Olive Veracruzana (page 146), the Mexican Roast Chicken with Crispy Skin (page 134), and the Cauliflower Rice Biryani (page 123).

MAKES 1 CUP [226 G]

1 large hothouse cucumber, peeled and seeded

½ cup [120 g] plain Greek yogurt

1 Tbsp extra-virgin olive oil

½ tsp ground coriander, toasted

¼ tsp ground cumin, toasted

¼ tsp kosher salt

Grate the cucumber on a box grater, then use a towel or cheesecloth to squeeze out all the liquid. Add the cucumber to a medium bowl along with the yogurt, olive oil, coriander, cumin, and salt. Stir well to combine. Store leftovers in an airtight container in the refrigerator for 1 day.

Kachumber GF DF V

While this has a kind of compli-cated name, think of kachumber as the Indian version of pico de gallo. Just as in Mexico where you'll find pico de gallo at every taco stand, you'll find this kachumber served with dosas and street food in India. It's a fresh, crunchy condiment that goes with everything. I espe-cially like it on my Lean Brisket Tacos (page 140), but it would be terrific on Lamb Salad with Guajillo Chile and Paleo 1000 Island Dressing (page 83), with Aromatic Everyday Cauliflower Rice (page 156), or Cauliflower Rice Biryani (page 123).

MAKES 1½ CUPS [340 G]

2 plum tomatoes, cored, seeded, and finely chopped

½ hothouse cucumber, peeled, seeded, and finely chopped

½ small jalapeño, seeded and minced

¼ small red onion, diced

1 Tbsp chopped cilantro (stems and leaves)

1 Tbsp fresh lime juice

¾ tsp kosher salt

Combine all the ingredients in a medium bowl and toss together. Store leftovers in an airtight container in the refrigerator for 1 to 2 days.

Mango Chutney ^{GF DF V}

I was recently interviewed for a story and asked what my guilty pleasures are, and one of them is, well, ketchup. Ketchup is loaded with sugar; it's almost like drinking soda. I really don't allow myself to use it. I tend to amp up my meals with chutneys instead. They live in this sweet, sour, and salty flavor space that is similar to ketchup, but they are much more healthful. A typical Indian meal always has a couple of chutneys on the table, and this mango one is definitely a favorite of mine.

MAKES 1½ CUPS [340 G]

½ tsp kosher salt,
plus more for blanching

½ small fennel bulb, diced

½ large, green (slightly unripe) mango, peeled and diced

2 Tbsp extra-virgin olive oil

1½ tsp ground coriander
(not toasted)

½ tsp ground fennel seeds
(not toasted)

¼ tsp cayenne (not toasted)

¼ tsp ground turmeric
(not toasted)

1½ tsp agave

First, bring a small pot of water to a boil and add enough salt so it is generously seasoned (1 to 2 Tbsp). Prepare a large bowl filled with water and ice. Add the fennel to the pot and blanch until just tender, about 2 minutes. Drain the fennel and place it in the ice bath (you could also run it under really cold water for a minute until the fennel is cold). Spread the fennel out on a paper towel and pat it dry.

Add the fennel and the diced mango to a medium bowl and set aside.

Next, in a small pan, gently heat the olive oil over low heat with the coriander, fennel seeds, cayenne, and turmeric. Stir the oil and spice mixture continuously until it is aromatic, 2 to 3 minutes. Add the oil and spices to the bowl of fennel and mango. Add the agave and salt and stir well. Leave to marinate for 30 minutes to 1 hour, after which it's ready to serve.

Store leftovers in an airtight container in the refrigerator for 3 to 5 days.

Coconut Chutney ^{GF DF V}

If you love coconut, you will fall hard for this traditional South Indian chutney. I like it with Cauliflower Rice Biryani (page 123), Black Chickpeas and Lentils with Spinach (page 120), Saag (page 168), and always with Gluten-Free Roti (page 45).

MAKES 1 CUP [226 G]

½ cup [113 g] ground unsweetened coconut

1 Tbsp coconut oil

3 medium garlic cloves, minced

1 in [2.5 cm] piece fresh ginger, peeled and minced

½ small Spanish onion, minced

1 tsp black mustard seeds, toasted

½ cup [120 ml] coconut milk

Small pinch of ground cinnamon, toasted

¼ tsp kosher salt

First, in a large, dry, heavy-bottomed pan, toast the coconut over low heat. Stir constantly until it turns a light golden color. Transfer to an 8 by 16 in [20 by 40.5 cm] sheet tray and let cool on the counter.

Next, in a medium pot over medium heat, heat the coconut oil and add the garlic, ginger, and onion. Gently cook until aromatic and softened, 8 to 10 minutes. Add the ground coconut and mustard seeds and cook for another 3 to 5 minutes, until you can smell the coconut toasting. Add the coconut milk and cinnamon, stir to combine, cover with a cartouche (see page 129), and let cook until the liquid is absorbed. The chutney should be a paste-like consistency that holds together when formed into a ball. Season with the salt.

Store leftovers in an airtight container in the refrigerator for 3 to 5 days.

Eggplant and Roasted Pepper Ajvar GF DF V

This ajvar is based on a Croatian/Slovakian roasted eggplant sauce that is similar to a baba ghanoush. It's a fun and flavorful condiment that you can use as a dip for Seed Crackers (page 166), with crudité, or as a sandwich spread. This is great with the Baked King Salmon with XO Sauce (page 132), but it also works well with Gluten-Free Roti (page 45). You could also spread this on a Bison Burger (page 86) instead of the Balsamic Onions and Paleo 1000 Island Dressing.

MAKES 1½ CUPS [340 G]

1 large eggplant

1 large red bell pepper

1 small garlic clove

2 Tbsp extra-virgin olive oil

1 tsp red wine vinegar

1 tsp kosher salt

Preheat the oven to 400°F [200°C].

First, bake the whole eggplant (including the stem) in the oven for 50 to 60 minutes, until very soft.

Roast the red bell pepper directly over the flame of the stove or under the broiler until it becomes black all over, 10 to 15 minutes. Put the pepper in a small bowl and cover with plastic to steam the skin off the pepper. Once the pepper has cooled enough to handle and has steamed, about 15 minutes, gently peel away the skin, remove the stem and seeds, and set side.

When the eggplant is cool enough to handle, peel away the stem and skin and place the flesh in a fine-mesh sieve over a bowl to let the liquid drain out. This should take 30 to 40 minutes. The longer the eggplant sits, the more liquid will drain out.

Combine the roasted pepper, eggplant, garlic, olive oil, vinegar, and salt in a blender and purée for 3 to 4 minutes, scraping down the sides of the blender several times to make sure all the ingredients get fully incorporated.

Store leftovers in an airtight container in the refrigerator for 3 to 5 days.

Spicy Red Curry GF DF V

This is a delicious and versatile curry sauce that adds spice and life to all kinds of protein—fish, chicken, and meat. For a side dish, you can also pour this over sautéed, stir-fried, or roasted vegetables. I also like to toss raw veggies with this curry and bake them in a casserole dish with chickpeas to serve over rice. Finally, this sauce is fun over the Yuba Noodle Salad with Ginger Dressing and Raw Vegetables (page 81) instead of the Ginger Dressing.

MAKES 1¼ CUP [283 G]

2 Tbsp coconut oil

1 small garlic clove, minced

½ small Spanish onion, minced

2 chiles de árbol

1 small jalapeño or serrano chile, minced

2 plum tomatoes, cored, seeded, and roughly chopped

1 Tbsp red wine vinegar

1 Tbsp tamari

1 tsp Thai red curry paste

½ tsp ground coriander, toasted

½ tsp kosher salt

¾ cup [180 ml] coconut milk

8 fresh curry leaves

First, add the coconut oil to a medium pot over medium-low heat. Add the garlic and onion and cook until soft (don't let them color), 8 to 9 minutes. Add the chiles de árbol and jalapeño to the pan and cook for another 5 to 6 minutes, until just getting soft.

Next, add the tomatoes, vinegar, tamari, curry paste, coriander, and salt, and cook for 5 to 6 more minutes, until aromatic. Pour in the coconut milk, add the curry leaves, and bring to a boil. Turn down the heat to medium and simmer for 2 minutes so it starts to thicken slightly. Transfer to a blender and purée for 3 to 4 minutes, scraping down the sides of the blender several times to make sure all the ingredients get fully incorporated.

Store leftovers in an airtight container in the refrigerator for up to 1 week.

ACKNOWLEDGMENTS

Thank you to my family: Ela, Heidi Ross, Ammi, Abba, Akbar, Colleen and family, Rahat, Peter, Phupu, Phupa, Rafat, Farhat and families

Thank you to my book team: Andrea Strong, Joanna Zucker Knollmueller, Rica Allannic, David Black, Camaren Subhiyah, Vanessa Dina, Antonis Achilleos, Claire Gilhuly, Chronicle Books

Thanks to chefs and friends: Loretta Keller, Tom Colicchio, Marco Canora, David Chang, Damon Wise, Jonathan and Liz Benno, Ed Carew, James Tracey, Karen DeMasco, Seamus Mullen, Cruz Goler, Tyler and Jennifer Lyne, Ahti Snow, Robby Silk, Dr. Ken Silk, Tom Henrion, Dominic Serratore, David Kupersmith, Mark Stevens

And finally, to the Alta Calidad crew: Oneyda Ortega, Michael Wetherbee, Kevin Wong, Aaron Feldman, Erin Bellsey, Shom Chowdhuri, Nimitt Mankad

INDEX

Chronicle Books publishes distinctive books and gifts. From award-winning children's titles, bestselling cookbooks, and eclectic pop culture to acclaimed works of art and design, stationery, and journals, we craft publishing that's instantly recognizable for its spirit and creativity. Enjoy our publishing and become part of our community at www.chroniclebooks.com.